The Bluffton Expedition

The Bluffton Expedition

The Burning of Bluffton, South Carolina, During the Civil War

Jeff Fulgham

Published 2012 by Jeff Fulgham

Cover design by Triad Design Group, Bluffton, S.C. Front and rear cover photographs by Colin Czerwinski. Map from *Harper's Weekly*, November 30, 1861.

ISBN 978-1-105-77454-6

Contents

Acknowledgements

My endeavor to write *The Bluffton Expedition* would not have been possible without the encouragement, support, and assistance from others. In addition, I find it essential to point out that no work of history can be completed without utilizing the existing building blocks of preceding historians. Their written words are a beacon that guides us through the difficult journey of historical research. The bibliography of *The Bluffton Expedition* documents this fascinating journey of more than two years.

I cannot thank historian Robert Jones, Jr. enough for his guidance throughout the editing process. Robert, who previously served as executive director of the Bluffton Historical Preservation Society, was uniquely qualified to assist with *The Bluffton Expedition*. Robert conducted an exhaustive historical content edit of each chapter, not only ensuring accuracy, but also providing valuable thoughts and suggestions from his vast knowledge of the subject. He was a pleasure to work with and I'll always treasure our analytical discussions and insightful examinations throughout the project. Robert's energy and enthusiasm is equaled by his professionalism and skill as a historian.

Donna Huffman will always hold a special place in my collective memories of the book. It was

Donna whom I originally contacted when I decided to write *The Bluffton Expedition.* Without hesitation she encouraged me and immediately began providing helpful ideas and suggestions. As the former president of the Bluffton Historical Preservation Society and owner of *Bluffton Breeze Magazine,* she offered a singular perspective with farsighted guidance. Donna discovered several treasured sources and nineteenth-century maps, which proved to be the key to understanding Bluffton's geographical divisions and landmarks in the 1800s.

Maureen Richards, Executive Director of the Bluffton Historical Preservation Society, deserves special thanks for always providing access to archival resource materials with enthusiastic accommodations. Maureen and her staff, including Susan Scoggins and Erin Dyer, were always eager to offer assistance during my visits to the Heyward House Historic Center located on Boundary Street in Old Town Bluffton. I was kindly given an informative tour of the Heyward House Museum on two occasions while conducting research. Their assistance was invaluable.

Spanning the vast period of our state's rich military history, The South Carolina Military Museum, located at the National Guard's Bluff Road Armory in Columbia, offers educational services and stunning exhibits and displays. Directing a friendly and professional staff, curator Ewell G. Sturgis, Jr. and numerous board members and advisors have acquired a premier selection of articles. Viewing the museum's Civil War collection, ranging from artillery pieces to authentic uniforms and accessories, was an enlightening experience and an absolute requisite for research.

The New York State Military Museum and Veterans Research Center provided several resources on the 48th New York Infantry as well as the John G. Abbott Diary. I'm grateful for their diligent efforts to make available such valuable historical data on their conveniently laid-out website.

Tommy Hopson, Sr., a longstanding member of The Church of the Cross and one of Bluffton's finest citizens, provided several official military records as well as his enlightening insight on the topic. I'm very appreciative for his interest in the story and his encouragement.

The assistance I received from author Neil Baxley was instrumental. Neil kindly made himself available to facilitate my understanding of the 11th South Carolina Infantry and its role in the war. Mr. Baxley has conducted extensive studies on the regiment including Company E, which was camped in Bluffton for much of the war. Neil's knowledge of the men and methods of the 11th South Carolina is unparalleled.

The recommendations of Chris Clayton, historian and President of the Lowcountry Civil War Roundtable, were crucial. His guidance on such topics as the Federal tariffs directed me to further examinations and a broader comprehension of the issues that catapulted the North and South into armed conflict in 1861.

I owe a special thanks to Dr. Dean T. Koukos. Dr. Koukos graciously took the time to help me grasp the basics of Civil War medicine and its rudimentary applications. Our discussion was very helpful and I'm beholden for his shared expertise.

From inception to completion, Bluffton Town Councilman Ted Huffman played an intrinsic role in the writing of *The Bluffton Expedition*. Ted kindly made himself available throughout the project, offering direction and advice in countless areas. Innumerable gatherings were spent discussing book sources and related geography while relishing a plate of Ted's famous Bluffton BBQ. Ted's unwavering support was absolutely vital.

The tireless labors of photographer and historian Mike Stroud have facilitated the research efforts of many authors including myself. Mike's work with the Historical Marker Database and other sites has simplified online exploration considerably.

As I consider the extent of the book's bibliography, I find it only fitting that in the closing stages of the editing process I would discover one last source to finalize the list. Thanks to my friend Richard Coffield, I was directed to a valuable addition to the collection which added significantly to my understanding of Bluffton during the Civil War.

The final draft would not have been possible without the wise counsel and helpful suggestions of an outstanding review team. My good friend of many years Christine Osler reviewed the first draft and her ideas improved the book considerably. She was instrumental in helping shape the chronological order of the story, which improved clarity and enhanced readability.

Corey Martin, a talented history teacher at Bluffton High School, reviewed the initial draft and made considerable contributions. Like all good teachers, Corey's analytical questions gave me a new perspective on my work, which helped to clearly define the type of book I was writing.

Garratt A. Williams, a longtime friend and wounded warrior who served in both Iraq and Afghanistan, offered several helpful suggestions. He accompanied me on vital research outings and was instrumental in efforts to clearly associate Civil War era sites with modern geographic descriptions. Garratt's notions also enriched the story by adding life to several of the subjects through the increased usage of primary sources.

The cover design was a project within its own right. The final creation was the result of several months of work that originated with my vision of an antique brass compass lying on a nineteenth-century map. After weeks of searching for and finally finding the precise map and compass, I garnered the assistance of a very talented young photographer, Colin Czerwinski. His striking photograph was the basis for the cover design. Rob Lembo and Christina Laios at Triad Design Group then worked to create the remarkable finished cover you see today. It was an immense pleasure working with everyone who contributed to the cover.

I would like to especially thank my family, friends, and fellow soldiers who supported my endeavor to write *The Bluffton Expedition*. I wish I could mention every one of you, but the list would be extremely long and I know I would fall short and fail to mention someone. Please know that I am indebted to each of you.

Finally, I will always be grateful to my immediate family, who experienced the toil of my research and writing on a regular basis. The majority of my spare time was spent immersed in the project, and their encouragement and support was critical to the completion of the book. *The Bluffton Expedition* would not have been possible without my remarkable and supportive wife, Paula, and two wonderful stepchildren, Colin and Taylor.

Preface

Over the years, fragments of the story of the burning of Bluffton were passed down orally from generation to generation in the local area. Tales of gunboats steaming up the winding May River and soldiers torching the town have echoed for nearly 150 years. I was eight years old when my mother initially told me a version of the Union expedition as we stood on the steep bluffs in Old Town. As the years and the tides gently passed, I often wondered about the accuracy of this lore, or oral tradition as we refer to it in historical terms.

The inquisitive nature of children is often refreshing to adults. As I reflect back to a much quieter time on the peaceful May River, I can now appreciate the intellectual probe of a young, simple boy, who sought answers concerning the small world around him. The idea to write *The Bluffton Expedition* emanated years later out of a natural passion for history as well as a practical need for answers. In November of 2009 I began conducting research on the burning of Bluffton. Two months later, in January of 2010, I contacted Donna Huffman, the former president of the Bluffton Historical Preservation Society, and apprised her of my plans to write the book.

My principal objective in writing *The Bluffton Expedition* was to tell the most accurate and concise story possible, based on solid historical records gathered from an array of primary and secondary sources. While I may have a passion for history, I realize how busy our lives can be with families and work. So from the outset the book was designed to be a brief history, in the hopes that even non-history enthusiasts would enjoy the story. In addition, it was important for me to create a book with adequate original maps and images, designed to facilitate the reader's journey through time. My love of history and affection for bringing the past to life is equaled by my interest in touring historical sites. Standing in the very location of those before us and observing the same homes, churches, and landscapes that existed 150 years ago is fascinating. If my book inspires just one individual to take a guided or self-guided historical tour of charming Old Town Bluffton, then I will consider it a success.

The Bluffton Expedition was intended to be a story about the significance of Bluffton during the Civil War, and more specifically what occurred on June 4, 1863, when two thirds of the town was destroyed by fire. Once I began conducting research, I immediately realized that the story could not be told effectively without including the basic outline of the Civil War in general, so during the course of the book I briefly include summaries of major and decisive battles and events throughout the states. These abstracts only serve to place the burning of Bluffton into context, however, as the detail is wrapped around the town itself.

Bluffton is a small town located in the heart of the beautiful South Carolina lowcountry. Spelled locally with one word, the lowcountry is a geographical region stretching along the Atlantic coast. Bluffton is situated between Savannah, Georgia, and Beaufort, South Carolina, lying on the mainland and across the Intracoastal Waterway from Hilton Head Island. Perched atop a high and picturesque bluff on the north bank of the scenic May River, historic Bluffton has a unique charm commonly associated with village environments. Although the town's population and area have grown considerably through multiple annexations in recent years, the historic original one square mile now referred to as Old Town has changed little in decades.

During most of the Civil War, civilians were absent from Bluffton, so this account is unique and is largely a story about the town and the Confederate and Union soldiers who fought in the area during the war. Conducting research and writing *The Bluffton Expedition* posed a number of challenges. Because the official records of the Union and Confederate militaries were written by officers who possessed nineteenth-century maps, becoming familiar with the Bluffton of yesterday required an extensive study of miscellaneous archival materials.

Identifying the specific whereabouts of certain documented incidents during Civil War operations was by far the most tedious and time consuming undertaking. For example, determining where an amphibious Union force landed on the Bluffton mainland in a particular expedition sometimes required the examination of unrelated writings by other officers from separate operations.

To make geographical surveys even more complicated, nineteenth-century maps were not always accurate. In addition, there are some instances, and understandably so, where officers erred slightly while recording distances between positions or reporting the names of specific places. Another challenge was establishing a timeline of events for the day Bluffton was burned. In a few circumstances officers or diary keepers recorded the exact times of certain incidents throughout the day. In most cases, however, I was required to calculate estimates based on several sources. As a result, the reader should be aware that most times are approximations.

Piecing together the events surrounding the burning of Bluffton was an intricate task. In the end, however, a holistic study of numerous documents, diaries, books, articles, and maps resulted in a fairly clear understanding of what occurred in Bluffton during the war, and more specifically, on the day when most of the town was destroyed by fire.

Having a passion for history, it was inevitable that I would eventually write *The Bluffton Expedition*. Hearing its oral history sparked my interest in bringing the past to life for the first time as I stood on the bluffs of the May River, trying to imagine the events that unfolded on the morning of June 4, 1863.

I

Antebellum Bluffton

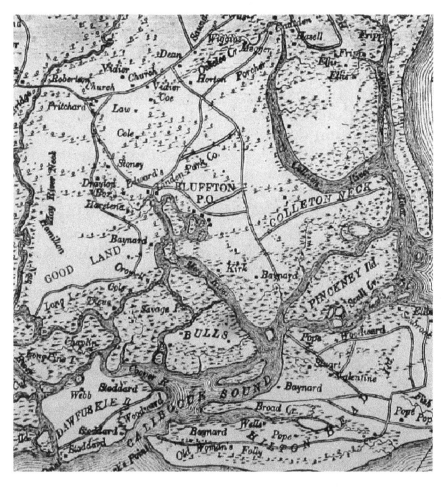

A portion of a circa 1870's map. Courtesy of the Bluffton Historical Preservation Society.

The foundations of antebellum Bluffton and the partitioning of neighboring plantations and parcels had only recently been established with the subdivision of the Devil's Elbow Barony. In 1718 the barony was granted to Sir John Colleton, the grandson of the first baronet (1608–1666) of the same name. The original baronet was one of the eight Lords Proprietors who had been granted the Province of Carolina in 1663 by King Charles II.[1] The Devil's Elbow Barony encompassed approximately 13,000 acres, and "...covered an area between the Colleton and Okatie Rivers on the north, the May River on the south, Mackay Creek on the east, and a line drawn from Linden Plantation on the May River to and including Rose Hill Plantation on the Okatie River..."[2]

Prior to 1777, the western portion of the barony was divided into several tracts and sold. "The 680 acre tract received by Benjamin Walls included most, if not all, of the area now covered by the town of Bluffton."[3] By the early 1800s, a small and alluring hamlet was established on the Walls Tract, situated on the northern bank of the May River in St. Luke's Parish. The parish was situated within Beaufort District, later to be designated as Beaufort County under the guidelines set forth by the state's postbellum constitution. "In Saint Luke's Parish in the 1820s, many planter families from Hilton Head and the adjacent mainland plantations began building modest summer resort cottages along the spectacular forty-foot bluff with a commanding view of a beautiful bend of the May River."[4]

At this time the community was mainly a pleasant retreat for the wealthy and was initially referred to simply as May River. By 1828 the last shares of the Devil's Elbow Barony were sold by the Colleton heirs, thus ending an enduring legacy. On September 25, 1828, as part of this auction, a local planter named James B. Kirk purchased Hunting Island Plantation, consisting of 946 acres and situated east of and adjacent to the community of May River. The western section of this plantation, which included today's Martin's Place, was referred to as Kirk's Bluff. The tiny hamlet of May River was thenceforth occasionally known as Kirk's Bluff as well.

Eventually the local residents met and agreed to name the small village Bluffton, in reference to its most prominent terrain feature. The existing layout of the village's original one square mile was purportedly staked out in the 1830s. Calhoun Street, leading to the May River, would become the heart of antebellum Bluffton and the center for its commercial activities.

Bluffton's healthful environment attracted planters who longed to evade the harsh and unhealthy conditions of the plantations, which were often situated adjacent to muggy, fertile bottomland. This was particularly the case for rice plantations located within the floodplains of rivers. This insalubrious setting, with its stagnant water and idle winds, spawned the detested malaria-carrying mosquitoes. The lack of screening on windows and porches during the antebellum era increased human contact with these pests, leading to higher occurrences of malaria.

Planter families would often migrate to their summer homes on the May River from surrounding plantations during the "sickly season" from May until the first frost. "Miasma was the name given to the environmental condition that occurred around the low lying plantations, especially rice plantations. With only a limited understanding of malaria and its causes at the time, it was thought that the fog, often developing at night during the warm months, was conducive to creating malarial or 'country fever' as it was then called."5 The threat of malaria was therefore always a looming concern for the inhabitants of the lowcountry.

In contrast to the still waters and inert winds of the rice plantations, the deep May River and its feeder coves flowed freely while its high bluffs faced the prevailing southern winds of summer. This predominant summer breeze fanning the north bank of the May River was much sought after and appreciated by the planters. Hot and stifling summer days were tolerable and even pleasant while residing at a cottage high atop the river's bluff.

The unhealthy conditions of the working plantations were not the only unfavorable settings in the lowcountry that made the May River so attractive to those who could afford a summer home there. "The urban environment had additional drawbacks too. Charleston and Savannah were considered less than healthful due to messy streets, lamp black from street lamps, foul smells from discharged garbage, and livestock that freely ran to and fro through the streets."6 These unsanitary conditions created a favorable environment for communicable diseases to spread throughout the cities, adding to the allure and desirability of May River and other comparable communities.

The summer homes established along the May River were characterized by certain design traits that had been adapted to meet the demands of the lowcountry, and were often raised above the ground on piers to provide adequate ventilation. In most cases, these clapboard-sided residences had large porches for casual living.

Several well-preserved examples of this vernacular form of lowcountry architectural design can still be viewed in some of Bluffton's remaining antebellum homes. The Cole-Heyward House is a splendid illustration. In the early 1840s, John J. Cole built this summer dwelling for his family on Boundary Street. Like many builders of the day, Cole chose plans for his home based on the early Carolina Farmhouse style of architecture, which was heavily influenced from the West Indies.[7] John and his wife Caroline Corley owned nearby Moreland Plantation located at May River Neck, or present-day Palmetto Bluff.[8]

As Bluffton's population growth mirrored that of the rest of the country in the early 1800s, so did its need for efficient modes of transportation and communication. While the steamboat and then the railway made America's westward expansion possible, Bluffton was limited to the assistance of the steamboat, as the railroad had not reached the town, and horse and wagon travel was slow and uncomfortable, especially for the sick or elderly.

The stagecoach road between Savannah and Bluffton was often muddy and rough as it traversed through swamp and marshland. The route was approximately 25 miles in length and the excursion could take anywhere between four to eight hours depending on the horse and the type of wagon if one was used, the four-passenger surrey being the most common. A ferry landing was situated near the confluence of the Back and Savannah Rivers across from the downtown district. A round trip to Savannah was often a three-day trek, consisting of two days' travel and one day's stay in the city.

The Cole-Heyward House, circa 1840s. Boundary Street, Bluffton. Photograph by Jeff Fulgham.

The value of the steamboat to Bluffton area residents during the antebellum period was immeasurable. A dock was soon built at the end of Calhoun Street and was used for both private and commercial activities, with a ferry service linking Bluffton and Savannah by 1843.[9] "From Bluffton's earliest days, commercial activity centered on this area where a wharf for docking packet boats and steamers laden with passengers, mail, and commercial goods unloaded. The local plantation products: rice, cotton, indigo, and naval stores were thence shipped to the regional ports of Savannah and Charleston for sale by factors dealing in goods bound for northern U.S. and European buyers."[10]

One of antebellum Bluffton's most historically significant events was the Bluffton Movement, which spawned from a political meeting held in the town on July 31, 1844. The movement arose out of a Southern protest against the Federal Tariffs of 1828 and 1842. Incensed Southerners commonly referred to the infamous 1828 tariff as the "Tariff of Abominations." These laws imposed a tax on imports, which proved costly to Southern planters who lacked the manufacturing capabilities of the North, and were often able to purchase goods from Europe cheaper than those from Northern factories.

The spokesman and leader of the Bluffton Movement was Beaufort native Robert Barnwell Rhett, who had served as a South Carolina State Representative from 1826 to 1832, and later as the state's attorney general. Rhett, a political extremist referred to as a "fire-eater," was elected to Congress in 1836, where he now staunchly opposed the federal tariff and pushed for the annexation of Texas as a slave state. "Rhett's increasingly impassioned speeches in favor of secession met with much favorable reaction among many of the planters of the Lowcountry and he was invited to address a group of his constituents in Bluffton."[11] This invitation resulted in the dinner party and political rally of July 31, 1844.

Although several days of consistent rain prior to the event hampered attendance, several hundred of Rhett's constituents still appeared at the gathering. Rhett gave his fiery and now legendary speech atop a platform that had been erected under the shade of a sprawling live oak, which would later be referred to as the Secession Oak.[12] "What Rhett was seeking to launch at Bluffton was a statewide political movement to call for an immediate state convention to nullify the Tariff of 1842, which had been raised again in violation of the Compromise of 1833, or for the immediate secession of South Carolina from the Union."[13]

R.B. Rhett's residence, Beaufort, S.C., circa 1861–1869. Library of Congress.

Live Oak Avenue, Robert B. Rhett's plantation, Port Royal Island, S.C. Library of Congress.

Most South Carolinians were not prepared to support such an extreme undertaking at the time. The popular and politically powerful John C. Calhoun, "South Carolina's giant elder statesman,"[14] was for a more moderate approach to the states' rights movement. When Calhoun passed away at age 68 in 1850, however, the more extreme secessionist movement spawned by Rhett and carried on by "The Bluffton Boys" was suddenly propelled in the absence of moderation and opposition.

"The Bluffton Boys" was a phrase that symbolized those who supported the movement, rather than a group of men exclusively from Bluffton. A few of the prominent supporters included John McQueen, William F. Colcock, Edmund Rhett, Whitemarsh B. Seabrook, and James Henry Hammond.[15]

Rhett continued to maintain a following in South Carolina long after the Bluffton Movement was hatched in 1844, and after serving 12 years in Congress he was elected by South Carolinians in 1850 to fill the United States Senate seat of the late Calhoun.[16] "Rhett held the seat barely a year, however, before resigning after South Carolina again backed away from secession as a result of protests over the compromise of 1850."[17] After his resignation, Rhett continued to fervently promote permanent separation from the Union. He went on to serve as a member of the South Carolina Secession Convention in 1860 and as a delegate at the Confederate's Montgomery Convention in February of 1861.

The historical impact of the Bluffton Movement was significant and the campaign garnered national attention. "History tends to show that 'The Bluffton Movement' did not subside but was a strong catalyst among the forces which brought about the secession of South Carolina on December 20, 1860..."[18] The movement had likely sown the first noteworthy seeds of secession in South Carolina, becoming so well known in political circles in Columbia and Washington that the term "Bluffton" was often used to describe the movement, rather than a proper noun describing the community.[19]

Bluffton's antebellum scene was one of extraordinary leisure and tranquility. Not only were the bulk of Bluffton's residents part of the "Planter Aristocracy," but the town itself was an escape from the general working environment of the agricultural estates. Unlike much of the surrounding area dominated by functioning plantations and populated by slaves and overseers, Bluffton's unhurried atmosphere made it a novelty for the planter class.

Antebellum life for most residents of the village was one of relative privilege as compared to that of the average southerner. Although calculations vary, we know that the majority of southerners did not own slaves. A widely accepted estimate reveals that around 25 percent of southerners owned slaves.[20] The greater part of landowners within antebellum Bluffton, however, would have fallen into the category of slave owners.

In the antebellum South, power and wealth were retained by a small segment of the populace. "In 1850, only 1,733 families [out of a white southern population of approximately 5.5 million] owned more than 100 slaves each, and this select group provided the cream of the political and social leadership of the section and nation."[21]

With such a concentration of fortune and political clout firmly in the hands of only a fraction of the general public, the antebellum South in many ways resembled an oligarchy, or a government controlled by a select few. "The planter aristocrats, with their blooded horses and Chippendale chairs, enjoyed a lion's share of Southern wealth. They could educate their children in the finest schools, often in the north or abroad. Their money provided the leisure for study, reflection, and statecraft."[22]

This relaxing lifestyle included abundant time for the sporting traditions of hunting and fishing, which were popular pastimes for plantation owners throughout the South. Hunting was done for both sport and regular sustenance on the large and sprawling plantations. The village of Bluffton was well known for its outstanding fishing along the May River and its adjacent creeks. Many of the same species of fish that are so enthusiastically sought after by sport fishermen today were pursued in the bygone antebellum days of the lowcountry.

Socializing played a prominent pastime in Bluffton as well, as most of the families residing in the village were well acquainted and visits were common. Sundays played a special role in the community as it did throughout the country, with many families worshiping at The Church of the Cross on Calhoun Street. The original chapel of this Episcopalian church was established in 1842 near the site of the current structure, which was completed in 1857. The first rector of The Church of the Cross was the Reverend James Stoney. "An advertisement in the Charleston Courier names Edward Blake White, who had designed other churches in Charleston and Columbia, as the architect."[23]

The town of Bluffton was incorporated by an act of the South Carolina General Assembly in 1852, and a second church was established on Boundary Street the following year. The Reverend George Allen directed the construction of this Methodist Episcopal Church. The Classical Revival building was designed with an elegant Greek temple–style portico.[24]

The Church of the Cross, completed in 1857. Calhoun Street, Bluffton. Photograph by Jeff Fulgham.

Education was an essential facet of life for the planters as well. May River Academy was established early on as planters began building their summer cottages along the river. The school was later operated by a distinguished professor from Scotland named Hugh Train, and the renowned Southern poet Henry Timrod was one of the academy's instructors for several years prior to 1860.[25] When Timrod arrived in Bluffton he described the town as being a significant community with numerous homes. In a letter written to his sister Emily, Timrod spoke of his favorite leisure activity: "My usual afternoon's exercise however is a walk on the Bluff, or the wood behind Bluffton."[26]

Throughout the 1850s and during Timrod's teaching stint in Bluffton, the Southern plantation economy of the South Carolina lowcountry continued to thrive. "In fact, it was probably the most prosperous time in a history that was already 350 years old by the middle of the nineteenth century."[27] This powerful economic engine was fueled by the plantation system including its flourishing rice and cotton production. The small village of Bluffton shared in this remarkable and burgeoning prosperity with the remainder of Beaufort District and the surrounding lowcountry.

As the plantation system became more and more vigorous, however, ideological and political differences between the North and South continued to fester. The splitting cultural divide at the Mason-Dixon Line grew more definitive, and calls for secession increased to a feverish pitch. "The slavery question continued to churn the cauldron of controversy throughout the 1850s. As moral temperatures rose, prospects for a peaceful political solution to the slavery issue simply evaporated."[28] By 1860, it was gravely apparent that the country was plummeting in a downward spiral towards armed conflict.

Bluffton's Methodist Episcopal Church built in 1853, currently Campbell Chapel AME, Boundary Street, Bluffton. Photograph by Jeff Fulgham.

Seven Oaks, circa 1850, Calhoun Street, Bluffton. Photograph by Jeff Fulgham.

A view of the May River from the grounds of The Church of the Cross. May River Neck, or present-day Palmetto Bluff, is seen in the distance. Photograph by Jeff Fulgham.

Chapter I Source Notes

1. Henry Smith, "The Baronies of South Carolina," *The South Carolina Historical and Genealogical Magazine* (Volume 13, July, 1912, Number 3), 120.

2. *A Longer Short History of Bluffton, South Carolina* (Bluffton, S.C.: Bluffton Historical Preservation Society, Inc., 1988), 6.

3. *A Short History of the Early Days of Bluffton, South Carolina* (Bluffton, S.C.: Bluffton Historical Preservation Society, Inc., 1983), 4.

4. Lawrence S. Rowland, Alexander Moore, and George C. Rogers, Jr. *The History of Beaufort County, South Carolina: Volume 1 1514–1861* (Columbia, S.C.: University of South Carolina Press, 1996), 384.

5. Robert S. Jones, Jr. "Going to the Salt," *Coastal Angler Magazine* (January 2011).

6. Robert S. Jones, Jr. "Going to the Salt," *Coastal Angler Magazine* (January 2011).

7. *A Longer Short History of Bluffton, South Carolina* (Bluffton, S.C.: Bluffton Historical Preservation Society, Inc., 1988), 20.

8. *A Guide to Historic Bluffton* (Bluffton, S.C.: The Bluffton Historical Preservation Society, Inc., 2007), 20.

9. *A Longer Short History of Bluffton, South Carolina* (Bluffton, S.C.: Bluffton Historical Preservation Society, Inc., 1988), 8.

10. *A Guide to Historic Bluffton* (Bluffton, S.C.: The Bluffton Historical Preservation Society, Inc., 2007), 24.

11. *A Short History of the Early Days of Bluffton, South Carolina* (Bluffton, S.C.: Bluffton Historical Preservation Society, Inc., 1983), 9.

12. William C. Davis, *Rhett: The Turbulent Life and Times of a Fire-Eater* (Columbia, S.C.: University of South Carolina Press, 2001), 199.

13. Lawrence S. Rowland, Alexander Moore, and George C. Rogers, Jr., *The History of Beaufort County, South Carolina: Volume 1 1514–1861.* (Columbia, S.C.: University of South Carolina Press, 1996), 421.

14. Lawrence S. Rowland, Alexander Moore, and George C. Rogers, Jr., *The History of Beaufort County, South Carolina: Volume 1 1514–1861.* (Columbia, S.C.: University of South Carolina Press, 1996), 421.

15. Manisha Sinha and Junius P. Rodriguez, ed., *Slavery in the United States: A Social, Political, and Historical Encyclopedia Volume One* (Santa Barbara, CA: ABC CLIO, Inc., 2007), 197.

16. William C. Davis, *Rhett: The Turbulent Life and Times of a Fire-Eater* (Columbia, S.C.: University of South Carolina Press, 2001), xi.

17. William C. Davis, *Rhett: The Turbulent Life and Times of a Fire-Eater* (Columbia, S.C.: University of South Carolina Press, 2001), xi.

18. *A Longer Short History of Bluffton, South Carolina* (Bluffton, S.C.: Bluffton Historical Preservation Society, Inc., 1988), 12.

19. C. Vann Woodward, *Mary Chesnut's Civil War* (Published in the United States of America, 1981), 232.

20. Tim McNeese, *America's Civil War* (Dayton, OH: Milliken Publishing Company, 2003), 9.

21. David M. Kennedy, Elizabeth Cohen, and Thomas A. Bailey, *The American Pageant, Volume 1. To 1877* (Boston: Houghton Mifflin Company, 2006), 351.

22. David M. Kennedy, Elizabeth Cohen, and Thomas A. Bailey, *The American Pageant, Volume 1. To 1877* (Boston: Houghton Mifflin Company, 2006), 351.

23. *A Longer Short History of Bluffton, South Carolina* (Bluffton, S.C.: Bluffton Historical Preservation Society, Inc., 1988), 16.

24. *A Longer Short History of Bluffton, South Carolina* (Bluffton, S.C.: Bluffton Historical Preservation Society, Inc., 1988), 24.

25. Lawrence S. Rowland, Alexander Moore and George C. Rogers, Jr., *The History of Beaufort County, South Carolina: Volume 1 1514–1861*

(Columbia, S.C.: University of South Carolina Press, 1996), 384.

26. Walter Bryan Cisco, *Henry Timrod: A Biography* (Cranbury, N.J.: Rosemont Publishing and Printing Corp. Associated University Presses, 2004), 61.

27. Lawrence S. Rowland, Alexander Moore and George C. Rogers, Jr., *The History of Beaufort County, South Carolina: Volume 1 1514–1861* (Columbia, S.C.: University of South Carolina Press, 1996), 420.

28. David M. Kennedy, Elizabeth Cohen and Thomas A. Bailey, *The American Pageant, Volume 1 To 1877* (Boston: Houghton Mifflin Company, 2006), 409.

II

Opening Shots

Abraham Lincoln, circa 1863, by Mathew B. Brady.
National Archives and Records Administration.

With an atmosphere of impending doom lingering over Washington, Abraham Lincoln placed his hand on the Holy Bible and swore upon the presidential oath of office on March 4, 1861. Tensions had been escalating between Northern and Southern states for a number of years over crucial ideological differences.

Controversial disputes had rankled and dissolved the bonds between the two sections. These matters included slavery, states' rights, the 1828 and 1842 Federal tariffs, and the annexations of Texas and Oregon. In addition, "Bleeding Kansas" had become a battleground over the question of slavery. A prelude to war had emerged when pro-slavery proponents and abolitionists poured into the Kansas Territory, with bloody clashes between these groups erupting in 1856. The fight over whether the territory would become a slave or free state ended when Kansas was admitted to the Union as a free state on January 29, 1861.[1]

With a growing Northern population, coupled with the addition of anti-slavery states, the South feared that a politically dominant North would soon follow. Southerners were apprehensive of the spread of the abolitionist movement and its certain threat to the plantation system and their way of life. One by one the states had begun to secede.

By Lincoln's Inauguration Day, seven states had already seceded from the Union, South Carolina being the first to withdraw on December 20, 1860. Following the Palmetto State's lead was Mississippi, Florida, Alabama, Georgia, Louisiana, and Texas. The separated states then called for a convention at Montgomery, Alabama, in early February of 1861 and elected Jefferson Davis, a U.S. Senator from

Mississippi, as president of the provisional Confederate States of America. Davis was sworn in on February 18.

The State House in Montgomery, Alabama, where the provisional Congress of the Confederacy met on February 4, 1861. Harper's Weekly.

Jefferson Davis, circa 1860, by Mathew B. Brady. Library of Congress.

As the Southern states broke ties with the Union, they commandeered all federal property within their borders. "When Lincoln took office, only two significant forts in the South still flew the Stars and Stripes."[2] The most noteworthy of these was Fort Sumter.

Fort Sumter was located at the mouth of Charleston Harbor, guarding one of the most vital ports along the east coast of the United States. Designed with an irregular pentagon shape and high walls protruding from the water, the fort was an intimidating sight to any vessel approaching the harbor from the Atlantic Ocean.

Fort Sumter was situated on a manmade island, and had been under construction since 1829. By the turbulent year of 1860, the fort was near completion. It had been occupied by Union troops since the night of December 26, 1860, when Major Robert Anderson moved his force of 85 officers and men to Sumter from nearby Fort Moultrie on Sullivan's Island. Anderson's decision to transfer resulted from a tactical assessment, concluding that Fort Sumter was more defensible than Moultrie because it was remote and required fewer troops to man its fighting positions.

In January, Union officials informed President Lincoln that provisions for Sumter's 85-man garrison would be depleted by mid-April. With mounting dissidence and rumors of war circulating throughout the streets of Charleston, all eyes were now upon Fort Sumter with the arrival of April. Lincoln carefully deliberated on a method to resupply the Union garrison without provoking war.

His strategy was to convince Southern officials that he merely intended to replenish the fort with the necessities required to sustain the troops, rather than delivering arms, ammunition, and reinforcements.

"On April 8, 1861, President Lincoln informed Governor Pickens that provisions were being sent to Fort Sumter by water."[3] With Union ships en route, Brigadier-General Pierre G.T. Beauregard was directed by the Confederate government to issue an ultimatum to Major Anderson. Beauregard, West Point's former superintendent and a native of Louisiana, had recently resigned in order to serve the Confederacy. By way of messenger, Brigadier-General Beauregard now served Major Anderson a mandate on April 10: surrender or prepare for an assault. Then, at approximately 4:30 a.m. on April 12, 1861, after Anderson's refusal to surrender the fort, Confederate batteries opened fire on Fort Sumter in Charleston Harbor.

From her home in Charleston, the now famous diary keeper Mary Boykin Chesnut recalled: "At half-past four the heavy booming of a cannon. I sprang out of bed, and on my knees prostrate I prayed as I never prayed before."[4] As the bombardment of Sumter raged on, President Lincoln was simultaneously receiving telegraph messages imparting the latest updates. After an intense and overwhelming Rebel shelling, Anderson surrendered the fort at 2:30 p.m. on April 13, and soon the Confederate flag was flying above Fort Sumter.

After the surrender, Mary Boykin Chesnut witnessed two Confederate officers, one of whom was her husband, approaching on foot along the street. The officers were followed by a cheerful mob: "The crowd was shouting and showing these two as messengers of good news. They were escorted to Beauregard's headquarters. Fort Sumter had surrendered."[5]

According to historian Stephen B. Oates, the news from Charleston Harbor sent Lincoln into a solemn disposition. "Lincoln announced to his cabinet that the Rebels had fired the first shot, forcing on him the decision of immediate dissolution, or blood."[6] The president then mobilized 75,000 militiamen and called for a special session of Congress. "The shelling of the fort electrified the North, which at once responded with cries of 'Remember Fort Sumter' and 'Save the Union.'"[7]

A gaping cultural rift originating at the Mason-Dixon Line had officially plunged the United States into a long anticipated, and much dreaded civil war. On April 17, 1861, Virginia became the eighth state to secede from the Union. Two days later, Lincoln issued a blockade proclamation against Southern ports in South Carolina, Georgia, Florida, Alabama, Louisiana, Mississippi, and Texas. Then on April 27, the president announced an updated proclamation to include the states of Virginia and North Carolina.

According to the Commander in Chief, the extended blockade was for reasons mirroring the former: "And whereas, since that date, public property of the United States has been seized, the collection of the revenue obstructed, and duly commissioned officers of the United States, while engaged in executing the orders of their superiors, have been arrested and held in custody as prisoners, or have been impeded in the discharge of their official duties without due legal process."[8] By May 20, Arkansas, Tennessee, and North Carolina had formerly withdrawn from the Union as well.

Fort Sumter, 1861. Harper's Weekly.

The stage was now fixed for a clash of epic proportions. A total of 11 states had taken up arms to form the Southern Confederacy, with 23 sustaining the precarious Federal Union. The North possessed a superior industry, rail system, and a powerful navy, while the Confederate fleet was non-existent. The population of the Union equaled 22 million, the South numbered just 9 million, of which 3.5 million were slaves.

As Northern war planners began discussing various military strategies, General-in-Chief Winfield Scott proposed a basic outline that was appropriately dubbed the Anaconda Plan. The design called for a strangulating blockade of all Southern ports along the east and gulf coasts, taking full advantage of the Union's extensive and potent naval fleet. Additionally, Scott suggested inserting large numbers of troops south along the Mississippi River in an effort to cut and divide the South in two halves, east and west, thereby isolating Texas, Louisiana, and Arkansas.

By June, Lincoln had prudently formed the Blockade Strategy Board, which consisted of four knowledgeable members and was led by Captain Samuel Francis DuPont. The task of the commission was to further develop and refine the North's strategy of blocking and seizing vital ports along the Southern coast.

As DuPont's committee made necessary preparations for carrying out the Anaconda Plan, the Northern and Southern armies, freshly organized and drilled, geared up for their first major clash. "On 16 July 1861, the largest army ever assembled on the North American continent up to that time marched from the vicinity of Washington, D.C., toward Manassas Junction, thirty miles to the southwest."[9] This Union force, amounting to 35,000 soldiers, was commanded by Brigadier-General Irvin McDowell. On July 21, near a meandering creek known as Bull Run, McDowell would meet a nearly equal adversarial host of 32,000 Confederates led by Brigadier-General P.G.T. Beauregard and General Joseph E. Johnston.

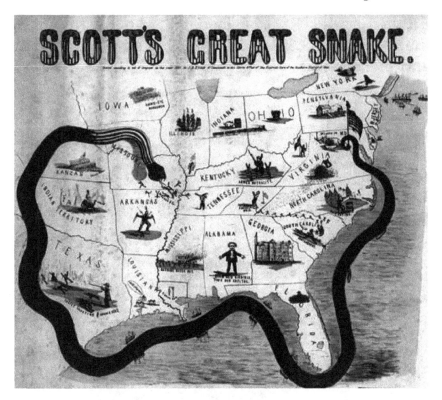

Scott's Anaconda Plan. Library of Congress.

Ultimately, the North suffered as a consequence of several delays in their attempts to reach the battlefield at critical times. Although both antagonists were mutually inexperienced and their movements awkward, the Confederates' efforts proved victorious. The Rebel leadership had been particularly effective in utilizing the railroad to transport companies to the front. "Johnston's decision to transport his infantry to the battlefield by rail played a major role in the Confederate victory."[10] Out of the 18,000 combatants engaged on either side, the opposing armies suffered equally with just over 1,700 casualties each. As the Union army quickly retreated and limped away from the

Battle of Bull Run, it became soberly apparent that America's Civil War would be agonizingly long and bloody.

Rear-Admiral Samuel Francis DuPont, circa 1863. Courtesy of the U.S. Naval Historical Society.

Following Lincoln's call for 75,000 troops to be mobilized in April of 1861, and prior to the Battle of Bull Run, the 48th New York Infantry Regiment began its formation in Brooklyn. Abraham J. Palmer, a private who served with Company D, was chosen after the war by his comrades to author a book chronicling the regiment's history. Their prolonged narrative began when several officers and community supporters rented a room in Brooklyn and began advertising for recruits with the goal of raising a company-size unit. With immediate success in achieving the numbers of men required, the recruiters pushed on in an effort to build a regiment of approximately 1,000 men.

The officer chosen to command the regiment, which would at first be referred to as the "Continental Guard," was the pastor of the Pacific Street Methodist Episcopal Church in South Brooklyn. Dr. James H. Perry had attended West Point for three years before accepting a commission as colonel and joining Texas in its fight for independence against Mexico. When asked by several members of the community if he would consider serving the Union after Lincoln's call to mobilize an army, Perry responded: "I have given the matter careful consideration. Our country needs help; there are dark and serious days before it, and this rebellion must be crushed..."[11]

Dr. Perry went on to explain that if the recruiters could successfully enlist an adequate number of men, he would willingly accept the commanding position. Colonel Perry and Lieutenant-Colonel William B. Barton, along with Quartermaster Irving M. Avery, thereby began the formation of the "Continental Guard," later to be officially mustered into service as the 48th Regiment, New York State Volunteers.

As the 48th New York was answering Lincoln's call to arms, the South was shaping its militias and erecting an army as well. A few months after South Carolina's prompt departure from the Union, "...the South Carolina Legislature immediately passed an Act requiring that ten regiments of infantry be raised for the defense of the state."[12] Each regiment would consist of ten individual companies comprised of 100 men each. The bill was signed into law by South Carolina Governor Francis W. Pickens, and the extensive undertaking of organizing the militias and merging the states to create a composite Confederate army was underway.

"Among the regiments raised in those first months of 1861 was the 9th South Carolina Volunteers."[13] The regiment's numerical designation was changed to the 11th during reorganization when it was discovered that two contingents within South Carolina had erroneously been designated the 9th. The regiment was formed under the leadership of Colonel William C. Heyward, a lowcountry planter who had been appointed by Governor Pickens. Colonel Heyward organized the 11th from a central location in Hardeeville, with specific companies assembling at surrounding sites.[14]

Company E, known as the "Hamilton Guards," officially mustered into service on June 24, 1861, at Bay Point in Port Royal Sound. The company was commanded by Captain Middleton Stuart and consisted of men from Beaufort and Barnwell Districts, and would eventually be stationed in

Bluffton along the banks of the May River for much of the war. As Company E and the 11th South Carolina Infantry readied throughout the summer of 1861 for a conceivable Union invasion, the 48th New York was expanding its rosters and preparing for deployment.

Colonel James H. Perry, circa 1861. Library of Congress.

The date of July 24, 1861, was noteworthy for the 48th New York, for on this day the first recruits entered camp and began training at Fort Hamilton, Long Island. Their bivouac site within the fort was named Camp Wyman, in honor of a citizen of Brooklyn, Luther B. Wyman, who had been a key patron of the regiment. The administrative roll books thickened over the next few weeks as new enlistees continued to trickle into the camp.

The boys in blue had volunteered to fight for various reasons. Some desired to maintain the Union, while others served out of a sense of loyalty and duty, as did many Southern recruits. Many of the young men who entered Camp Wyman were only youths in the 1850s, when introduced to the injustices of slavery through the literary work of Harriet Beecher Stow's *Uncle Tom's Cabin.* "The tale was devoured by millions of impressionable youths in the 1850s, some of whom later became the boys in blue who volunteered to fight the Civil War through to its grim finale."[15]

On the afternoon of July 30, 1861, a young recruit from New Jersey named John G. Abbott arrived at Camp Wyman. He had left home on July 25 to join the boys in blue. Upon reaching the camp, his first task was to assist others in pitching a tent: "In the afternoon went to Camp Wyman and put up the first tent and stayed at G.W. Gooddell in Brooklyn."[16] John had decided to keep a detailed record of his experiences in the war. This perceptive young man's remarkable diary would one day become recognized as a significant contribution to the annals of American Civil War history. At the encampment, Abbott and the other recruits continued to lay straw and erect numerous tents for the regiment: "Put up 50 more tents and went to Brooklyn with John Doering after straw for the camp."[17]

In the preliminary phase of training, the new recruits were drilled by their sergeants to instill discipline and encourage teamwork, both critical components of unit cohesion. The officers spent much of their time inspecting the troops, studying tactics, and further developing their understanding of the military strategies of the era. On August 16, 1861, the first few companies of the regiment were officially mustered into service by New York Governor Edwin D. Morgan.

While the 48th New York Infantry vigorously prepared for inevitable conflict, their counterparts in South Carolina did likewise. As the much-awaited season of autumn drew near in the sultry lowcountry, the commander of the 11th South Carolina Infantry, Colonel William C. Heyward, primed his lean soldiers for an imminent and pivotal battle.

After the formation of individual companies was accomplished, and the mobilization process completed, the members of the 48th New York began the initial leg of their extended journey south. First they boarded a ship and steamed from Fort Hamilton to South Amboy, New Jersey, on September 17. From there the soldiers were transported by rail to Philadelphia. From Pennsylvania they travelled to Baltimore and then Washington, where the weary troops bivouacked for two weeks on the grounds of Capitol Hill.[18]

On October 5 at 12:00 p.m., the regiment marched out of Washington, arriving in Annapolis, Maryland, at 11:00 p.m. that night. Then on

October 18 they boarded the ship *Empire City* and sailed to Hampton Roads, Virginia. Finally in late October, with the majority of the regiment aboard the *Empire City*, the 48th New York prepared to sail south for a secret destination, known only by a handful of high-ranking Union officials.[19]

The 48th would cruise with the newly formed South Atlantic Blockading Squadron, which had been assembled as a result of the efforts of the Blockade Strategy Board established in June. The mighty squadron was commanded by the newly promoted flag officer, Samuel F. DuPont.

In order to carry out an effective blockade along the southern coast, the Federal Navy would need a qualifying port and depot to establish a central base for operations. After a thorough examination of maps and charts of the shoreline for several months, President Lincoln and his board covertly decided on Port Royal Sound on the South Carolina coast. This deep and expansive harbor, conveniently located between the coastal cities of Charleston and Savannah, would offer the Union a valuable seaport to carry out Scott's Anaconda Plan.

After lengthy preparations, the huge squadron totaling 77 vessels, "the largest fleet yet assembled under the U.S. flag...,"[20] finally set sail on October 29. The flotilla's undisclosed destination of Port Royal Sound was issued to the ships' captains in sealed envelopes prior to departure.

Like the other members of the 48th New York aboard the *Empire City*, John G. Abbott was unaware of the expedition's endpoint. In his October 29 diary entry, Abbott recalled: "The fleet started at 7 o'clock. The Wabash leading. Passed

Capes Charles and Henry at 10 o'clock quite smooth. At 12 o'clock met one of the Blockade and hospital ship. Out of sight of land at 4 o'clock. Passed Cape Hattras at 4 o'clock in the morning. Steering south east."[21]

Eventually the envelopes were opened by the ships' commanders and the previously concealed target of Port Royal was unveiled. As the members of the 48th New York settled into their cramped quarters for a lengthy voyage aboard the *Empire City*, the 11th South Carolina prepared for a possible invasion at Port Royal.

Chapter II Source Notes

1. David M. Kennedy, Elizabeth Cohen, and Thomas A. Bailey, *The American Pageant, Volume 1 To 1877* (Boston, MA: Houghton Mifflin Company, 2006), 413.

2. David M. Kennedy, Elizabeth Cohen, and Thomas A. Bailey, *The American Pageant, Volume 1 To 1877* (Boston, MA: Houghton Mifflin Company, 2006), 435.

3. Fort Sumter National Monument, Exhibit Text, February 2002, National Park Service. Visitor Education Center, Liberty Square, Charleston, S.C.

4. C. Vann Woodward, *Mary Chesnut's Civil War* (New Haven, CT: Yale, 1981), 46.

5. C. Vann Woodward, *Mary Chesnut's Civil War* (New Haven, CT: Yale, 1981), 49.

6. Stephen B. Oates, *With Malice toward None: A Life of Abraham Lincoln* (New York, N.Y.: HarperCollins, 1977), 287.

7. David M. Kennedy, Elizabeth Cohen, and Thomas A. Bailey, *The American Pageant, Volume 1 To 1877* (Boston, MA: Houghton Mifflin Company, 2006), 435.

8. "Southern Ports Blockade Proclamations," April 19 & 27, 1861.

9. Ted Ballard, *Battle of First Bull Run* (Washington, D.C.: Center of Military History, United States Army, 2004), v.

10. Ted Ballard, *Battle of First Bull Run* (Washington, D.C.: Center of Military History, United States Army, 2004), 35.

11. Abraham J. Palmer, D.D., *The History of the Forty-Eighth Regiment, New York State Volunteers in the War of the Union 1861–1865* (Brooklyn, N.Y.: Veterans Association of the Regiment, 1885), 2.

12. Neil Baxley, *No Prouder Fate: The Story of the 11th South Carolina Volunteer Infantry* (Bloomington, IN: AuthorHouse, 2005), 1.

13. Neil Baxley, *No Prouder Fate: The Story of the 11th South Carolina Volunteer Infantry* (Bloomington, IN: AuthorHouse, 2005), 2.

14. Neil Baxley, *No Prouder Fate: The Story of the 11th South Carolina Volunteer Infantry* (Bloomington, IN: AuthorHouse, 2005), 4.

15. David M. Kennedy, Elizabeth Cohen, and Thomas A. Bailey, *The American Pageant, Volume 1 To 1877* (Boston, MA: Houghton Mifflin Company, 2006), 410.

16. John G. Abbott's Diary, July 30, 1861.

17. John G. Abbott's Diary, August 7, 1861.

18. Abraham J. Palmer, D.D., *The History of the Forty-Eighth Regiment, New York State Volunteers in the War of the Union 1861–1865* (Brooklyn, N.Y.: Veterans Association of the Regiment, 1885), 11.

19. Abraham J. Palmer, D.D., *The History of the Forty-Eighth Regiment, New York State Volunteers in the War of the Union 1861–1865* (Brooklyn, N.Y.: Veterans Association of the Regiment, 1885), 14.

20. Jack Sweetman, *American Naval History: An Illustrated Chronology of the U.S. Navy and Marine Corps, 1775–Present* (Annapolis, MD: Naval Institute Press, 2002), 62.

21. John G. Abbott's Diary, October 29, 1861.

III

Civil War in the Lowcountry

From the Official Records of the Union and Confederate Navies.
Map circa 1861.

Port Royal Sound was guarded by two hastily built Confederate fortifications. Fort Walker was located on Hilton Head Island to the south, and Fort Beauregard was situated on Phillips Island to the north. The former, and more robust stronghold, had been named in honor of the Confederate States Secretary of War, LeRoy Pope Walker from Alabama. The latter received its name from the accomplished General P.G.T. Beauregard. Beauregard had commanded the provisional Confederate forces during the initial attack on Fort Sumter and then distinguished himself at the First Battle of Bull Run in Virginia.

The sprawling entrance to Port Royal Sound as it passes between these two islands is approximately two miles in width. At its broadest expanse the harbor stretches to nearly three miles, then tapering as it transitions into the Broad River.

Fort Walker, an earthen fortress that was located on the water's edge in present-day Port Royal Plantation, was commanded by Colonel William C. Heyward of the 11th South Carolina Infantry. Colonel R.G.M. Dunovant was in charge of the defenses across the sound at Fort Beauregard. From his headquarters on Hilton Head Island, Brigadier-General Thomas F. Drayton was assigned as commander of Confederate forces in the overall defense of Port Royal. General Drayton was a prominent lowcountry planter, civil engineer, and politician who had served as president of the Charleston and Savannah Railroad.[1]

The American Civil War has often been referred to as the Brothers War. There are copious accounts of siblings taking oaths of allegiance on opposite sides of the Mason-Dixon Line. As a chief example, General Drayton's brother, Commander Percival Drayton, had pledged allegiance to the Union and was now serving in the Federal Navy as captain of the USS *Pocahontas*. The *Pocahontas* was part of the menacing armada that steadily approached Port Royal Sound.

Brigadier-General Thomas F. Drayton, circa 1861.
U.S. Archives and Records Administration.

Commander Percival Drayton, circa 1864, by Mathew Brady. Library of Congress.

After experiencing turbulent seas and adversity along the course, the great squadron, led by DuPont's flagship, USS *Wabash*, began arriving off the coast of St. Phillips and Hilton Head Islands on November 3. Soon the leading vessels were sighted by Rebels on the islands, which included three companies of the 11th South Carolina stationed on Hilton Head. Company E, commanded by Captain Middleton Stuart, was manning the defenses at Braddock's Point on the southern tip of the island.[2] Emplaced at this site, situated in present-day Sea

Pines Plantation, was a small gun battery guarding the passage into Calibogue Sound.

As fall weather began to cool the South Carolina lowcountry, reports quickly spread from the islands to the towns of Bluffton and Beaufort that a mighty flotilla was materializing off the coast. After several days of weather delays and reconnaissance missions, in which Union gunboats tested the reactive fire of the forts and a few small Confederate gunboats, DuPont readied his fleet for battle.

The rear-admiral ordered his warships into the position of attack at 9:00 a.m. on the morning of November 7, 1861. DuPont's choice of date and time was based on several factors including tide tables, the position of several Rebel gunboats commanded by Commodore Josiah Tattnall, and Fort Walker's vulnerability on its flanks. On this cool lowcountry morning, the battle commenced at precisely 9:26 a.m. when a single shot rang out from a massive cannon at Fort Walker, followed immediately by a round from Fort Beauregard.[3] The USS *Wabash* swiftly countered the Rebel blasts. DuPont's fleet, which was circling in a counterclockwise, oval formation, eagerly joined the contest.

All eyes and ears throughout the region were now honed in on Port Royal Sound. In a thunderous contest of firepower that echoed for miles around, the Battle of Port Royal, nicknamed "The Day [of] the Big Gun Shoot" by local slaves,[4] was underway and raged on for over four hours. John G. Abbott of the 48th New York was aboard the *Empire City* anchored just off shore from Hilton Head Island. He and the other members of the 48th witnessed the decisive bout. In his November 7 diary entry John wrote: "...the Rebel battery on the left point [Fort Walker] opening fire on the Frigate Wabash. The Wabash returned the compliment immediately which continued with incessant firing for about four hours, when they [Rebels] thought that they had enough shells for dinner and retreated."[5]

At some point during the battle, several Union vessels fell out of DuPont's formation. As a result, these warships settled in a position north of Fort Walker near the mouth of Hilton Head's Fish Haul Creek. This vantage point presented the Union frigates with an enfilading fire. This superior angle enabled the Union vessels to apply the brunt of their barrage upon Fort Walker's exposed side, where the flanks were not adequately equipped with artillery. Concerning the fort's weakness, DuPont later wrote: "...and the flanks were but slightly guarded, especially on the north, on which side the approach of an enemy had not been looked for."[6]

The effective fire of DuPont's squadron soon overwhelmed Fort Walker's defenses. By 2:00 p.m. the Confederates had evacuated the decimated fort. The Rebels promptly retreated to the Jenkins Island Ferry point situated across from Buckingham Landing. As the soldiers in gray were still crossing to the mainland in various types of river crafts, a Federal party had already entered Fort Walker after storming the beaches of Hilton Head. "At twenty minutes after two Captain Rogers hoisted the flag of the Union over the deserted post."[7] On Phillip's Island, Confederate Colonel R.G.M. Dunovant ordered the withdrawal from Fort Beauregard as Colonel Heyward and his troops were vacating Fort Walker. Beauregard had sustained an intense shelling, but not as severe as Walker, which received a concentration of the armada's precise cannon fire.

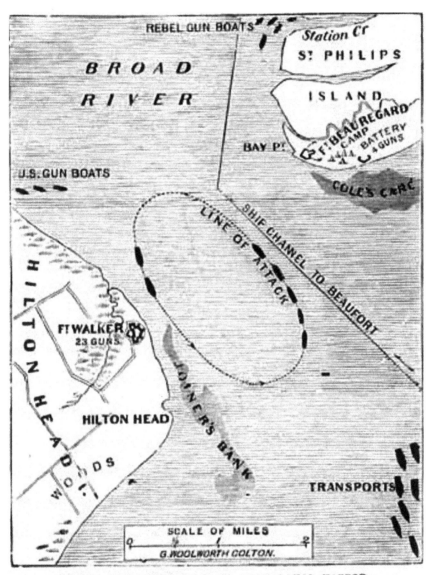

From the Official Records of the Union and Confederate Navies.
Map circa 1861.

Above, the "Great Expedition" and the attack on Forts Walker and Beauregard. Below, a scene from inside Fort Walker during the Battle of Port Royal. Harper's Weekly.

More than five vessels and their crews worked diligently throughout the night to transport more than 1,000 Rebels from Hilton Head to Buckingham Ferry. "At 1:30 a.m., by the aid of Commodore Tattnall's fleet, the steamers St. Johns and Edisto, and three large flats, capable of holding 150 men each, the troops were all safely embarked."[8] From Buckingham, many of the battered and fatigued Southerners treaded along Fording Island Road into the town of Bluffton.

Records indicate that more than 60 Confederate soldiers were either killed, wounded, or missing in action. The Union suffered relatively less, with 31 total casualties. In a dispatch to the Secretary of the Navy, Gideon Welles, flag officer DuPont wrote on November 8, 1861: "The defeat of the enemy terminated in utter route and confusion. Their quarters and encampments were abandoned without an attempt to carry away either public or private property."[9]

LANDING OF UNITED STATES TROOPS AT PORT ROYAL, AFTER THE BOMBARDMENT, NOVEMBER 7th, 1861.

The landing of Union troops on the beaches of Hilton Head Island, November 7, 1861. Harper's Weekly.

Retreat of the Confederate garrison from Fort Walker on Hilton Head Island, November 7, 1861, by Frank Leslie. Harper's Weekly.

From his newly established headquarters in Coosawhatchie, a 31-mile march north of Bluffton, General Robert E. Lee, who had now taken command of the Department of South Carolina, Georgia, and Florida, wrote to the Confederate Secretary of War, J. P. Benjamin. In this message composed on November 9, Lee summarized the outcome of the battle and informed Benjamin that General Drayton had transferred his command from Hilton Head to Bluffton.[10] Just as Drayton had utilized his island plantation home as his headquarters, it is probable that he set up this temporary command post at his summer home in Bluffton, situated at the northeast corner of Boundary and Water Streets, adjacent to Heyward Cove.[11] Drayton's halt in Bluffton was only momentary, however, as he soon shifted his command to Hardeeville.

The loss of Forts Walker and Beauregard were a major setback for the Confederates, who were now scattered and dispersed throughout the Bluffton and Beaufort areas. On the night of November 7, individuals and bands of soldiers who had been separated from their units in the hectic retreat staggered into Bluffton exhausted. Groups of now ill-equipped men huddled around campfires throughout the town, tending to the wounded and mourning the lost.

When the sun began to rise on the morning of November 8, the day after the fall of Hilton Head, the mainland and Bluffton in particular would now hold a novel and more strategic significance. Bluffton's few remaining citizens not involved in the war effort were evacuated at once. They fled inland to such towns as Grahamville, Gillisonville, and Allendale. The homes of Bluffton were now deserted with furniture and other belongings abandoned. Leisurely civilian strolls along Calhoun Street were a thing of the past. The sounds of laughter and children at play were now substituted with the marching orders of sergeants and the coordinated footsteps of soldiers.

Eventually the majority of Drayton's forces marched on to Hardeeville, while several companies established permanent camps in and around Bluffton. At around this time, the Rebels established an intricate network of lookouts surrounding the greater Bluffton peninsula to monitor Union activity.

The lookouts, or pickets as they were referred to, reported to a commander of outposts located in Bluffton. A series of couriers on horseback fused

Bluffton to Hardeeville, where a telegraph wire running contiguous with the Charleston and Savannah Railroad served as a communications link between the two cities. Horses ridden by cavalry lookouts trotted in and out of Bluffton as the troopers assumed or were relieved of their posts overlooking the surrounding waterways. But the town was void of women and children and other civilians. The chimneys in Bluffton's homes were damp and cold and the lanterns dark and without a glow.

Just across the intercoastal waterway, a continuous flow of Union troops had been landing on the beaches of Hilton Head Island since the afternoon of November 7. By November 9, five companies of the 48th New York had made landfall. On the afternoon of November 10, John G. Abbott set foot on the island's shore. Abbott noted in his diary: "Landed at the Fort [Walker] in South Carolina at 3 p.m. and then proceeded to camp which we found to be about one mile from the fort and in a cotton and corn field."[12] Within days of the fall of Fort Walker, approximately 13,000 Federal troops inhabited Hilton Head Island.

The reduction of forts Walker and Beauregard and the Union's occupation of Confederate territory were sobering and disturbing events for Southerners. The melodramatic cries for secession and independence that had bellowed from politicians like Robert Barnwell Rhett and others had brought about the harsh realisms of war. Moderate Southerners now more than ever regretted men like Rhett. The news bulletin emanating from Port Royal was a shock and a horror to South Carolinians.

Bluffton's national prominence as a hotbed of secessionist activity that emerged from the Bluffton Movement now played on the minds of many. After hearing the distressing reports concerning the Battle of Port Royal, Mary Boykin Chesnut penned her thoughts: "Bluffton must be satisfied now. It has about as much fighting on its hands as anybody need want— fire eaters [extremist politicians] or otherwise."[13]

Mrs. Chesnut was originally from the Charleston area and later lived near Camden, South Carolina. Her husband, James Chesnut, Jr., had served as a United States senator from South Carolina. After hearing the solemn news originating from Port Royal, Mary quoted Colonel James Chesnut, Sr., her elderly father-in-law: "For fifty years Bluffton has been spoiling for a fight. And now I think he has got it. That is the center spot of the fire eaters. Barnwell Rhetts and all that."[14]

With a victory at Port Royal, the Union navy had met its objective of establishing a strategic foothold and a vital port of operations. From this Southern harbor, the Federal Navy could initiate Scott's Anaconda Plan, which would place a smothering blockade on the Rebel coast. From this new base on Hilton Head Island, General Thomas West Sherman, a decorated veteran of the Mexican-American War who was appointed commander of the Department of the South, began focusing his energies on the Confederate-occupied city of Savannah and nearby Fort Pulaski. Thomas West Sherman is not to be confused with William Tecumseh Sherman of the noted "March to the Sea" from Atlanta to Savannah in 1864.

Mary Boykin Chesnut. From Mary Chesnut's Civil War.

Hilton Head Island gravesites of Union sailors killed during the Battle of Port Royal on November 7, 1861, by Timothy O'Sullivan. Library of Congress.

Situated on Cockspur Island at the mouth of the Savannah River and blocking access to the city, Fort Pulaski was a sturdy brick and mortar citadel that was completed in 1847. This robust fortress, located approximately five miles south of the southern tip of Hilton Head Island, was believed by some military experts to be invincible.

DRAYTON'S MANSION.

Hilton Head Island, S.C., circa 1862. From The History of the Forty-Eighth Regiment.

In December of 1861, the month following the Battle of Port Royal, Confederate forces, now aware of the Federal Navy's powerful and accurate guns, abandoned Tybee Island, Georgia. At around this time, General Sherman began taking full advantage of the lack of a Confederate presence on the island.

The Fort Pulaski siege plan developed by the Union called for severing the supply line to the fort's garrison and then surrounding Cockspur Island with newly established gun emplacements. The Union would slowly encroach on Cockspur Island by placing batteries on the nearby islands of Tybee, Long, Bird, and Jones. The heaviest concentration of artillery would be placed along the shoreline of Tybee Island to the east of Pulaski. In this effort, Daufuskie Island, located just three miles north of Cockspur Island, was used as a staging ground for troops involved in the siege works. "By January, 1862, Brigadier-General Egbert L. Viele was stationed on Daufuskie with several regiments of troops."[15] By the first week of February the units on Daufuskie consisted of: a detachment of the 3rd Rhode Island Artillery; a detachment of Volunteer Engineers; a battalion of the 8th Maine Regiment Volunteers; parts of the 6th and 7th Regiment Connecticut Volunteers; 28th Massachusetts; several companies of the 46th, 47th, and 48th New York Volunteers; and seven companies of the 3rd New Hampshire. Approximately 1,600 troops occupied Daufuskie at this time.

"Once on Tybee, General Thomas Sherman conceived the idea that it might be more advantageous to by-pass Fort Pulaski and make a direct attack on the city of Savannah."[16] In Sherman's opinion, circumventing Pulaski and attacking the city of Savannah directly was the wisest strategy and would bring the Union one step closer to dominance and victory in the South. A reconnaissance of the creeks along this proposed route to the north of the Savannah River was conducted by Rear Admiral DuPont to determine the feasibility of Sherman's proposed plan. DuPont's assessment was that the shallow depth of these creeks could possibly jeopardize the operation and leave an amphibious force stranded and vulnerable to enemy attacks.

The difference of opinion between these two high-ranking commanders on the best course of action began to negatively affect the cohesiveness of the Army's Department of the South and the Navy's South Atlantic Blockading Squadron. As a result, some historians believe that the friction resulting from the differing strategy proposals of DuPont and Sherman eventually led to Sherman's dismissal. Long before Sherman was relieved as commander of the Department of the South, however, he committed to the siege of Fort Pulaski: "On February 19 he [Sherman] sent his chief engineer, Captain Quincy A. Gillmore, to take command of all troops on Tybee Island and to prepare for the bombardment of Fort Pulaski."[17]

The strenuous toil of establishing Union batteries on the islands surrounding Pulaski continued. Because many of the heavy weapons needed to be traversed over mud and marsh to reach their effective positions, runways of wooden planks were built and laid to facilitate this movement. Much of the timber necessary for the planks was harvested from trees on Daufuskie Island. The overall effort and manual labor required of this task was so grueling that many Federal troops often collapsed from exhaustion. The soldiers were often buried to their knees and beyond in the pasty sludge while moving these cumbersome artillery pieces. Wearing sand bags over their feet to prevent the muck from filling their boots became a necessity. Most of this grueling work was carried out at night under cover of darkness in order to conceal the batteries' positions. In certain cases as many as 250 men were required to pull just one massive gun with large ropes across the marsh flats.

Sergeant John G. Abbott of the 48th New York, now camped on Daufuskie, had been assigned to these fatigue duties in preparations for the bombardment of Fort Pulaski. His diary entry for Tuesday, February 11, reads, "150 of our men went up to Jones Island at 4 PM. At 7 PM we commenced to pull the cannon, 6 of them, across to the Savannah, a distance of one mile. The mud was over knee deep. We got our supper at 11 o'clock that night. At 2 AM we succeeded in getting 2 of them in battery and the rest nearly across. We was all glad for morning to come."[18]

By the close of March, General Sherman's replacement had arrived. "On March 31 General Sherman was relieved of command of the Department of the South by Major-General David Hunter. Hunter, accompanied by General Benham, the district-commander, arrived on Tybee Island on the evening of April 8."[19] A graduate of the United States Military Academy and a former military paymaster, Hunter had been posted at Fort Leavenworth Kansas during the "Bleeding Kansas" struggle between abolitionists and pro-slavery proponents. He was considered by many to be one of the few abolitionists serving in the army officer corps during the pre-war struggle in Kansas.[20]

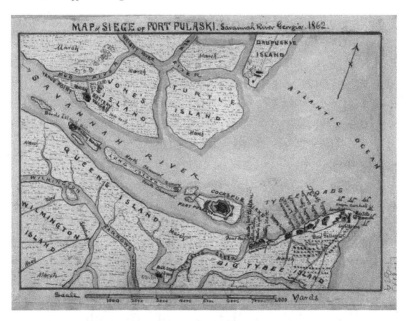

*Siege map of Fort Pulaski, 1862. Courtesy of the
Virginia Historical Society.*

*Union troops manually hauling a heavy artillery piece in preparation
for the bombardment of Fort Pulaski, 1862. Harper's Weekly.*

By April 7, final battle plans for the bombardment of Pulaski had been rehearsed, and the exhausting preparations of battery emplacements complete. Gun crews on the surrounding islands of Tybee, Long, Bird, and Jones, were now prepared to commence the offensive. With Captain Quincy Gillmore in command, the Union batteries were poised and ready for the attack.

At sunrise on the morning of April 10, 1862, Major-General Hunter sent word from Tybee Island to Cockspur Island demanding that Pulaski's commander surrender the fort. Confederate Colonel Charles H. Olmstead boldly and defiantly replied, "I am here to defend this fort, not to surrender it."[21] Shortly after Olmstead's refusal to surrender, Gillmore ordered his batteries to commence fire. Olmstead then directed Pulaski's cannons to respond. Just five months following the bombardment and subsequent collapse of Forts Walker and Beauregard in Port Royal Sound, the Rebel garrison at Fort Pulaski was now under a forceful and piercing barrage.

The heavy guns of both the aggressors and defenders remained active throughout the day with moderate damage inflicted on Pulaski's bulwarks. The Federal artillery pieces located on Tybee were mostly unscathed, as the majority of the emplacements consisted of resilient earthen mounds and sand bags.

With the arrival of nightfall, the explosive thundering of guns heard from miles around eventually tapered off. Throughout the night a consistent but less frequent exchange of fire echoed from Savannah to Hilton Head and beyond. On average, no more than about eight rounds were fired each hour until sunrise. This lull in activity enabled the Confederates to make much needed repairs throughout the night.

At sunrise on the morning of April 11, 1862, it was immediately apparent that a new day had dawned in the evolution of warfare. The damage to Fort Pulaski was overwhelming. As a result of the landmark arrival of the technologically advanced rifled artillery used by the Union, as opposed to the shorter ranged and less effective smooth bore, the southeast wall of the fort had been reduced to rubble. The penetrating power of the James Rifle repeatedly shattered the brick and mortar fortress. With each devastating blow to the wall of the fort, the rifled shell would penetrate as much as 20 to 25 inches. The lethal effectiveness of the James Rifle would be of monumental importance in the future design and construction of fortifications.

Sergeant John G. Abbott had witnessed the bombardment of Fort Pulaski from three miles away on Daufuskie Island. By 9:00 a.m. on April 11, the Confederate flag waving above the fort had been shot down on three occasions, and each time it had been replaced by the Rebels.[22] By midday, Union artillery shells began to threaten the northwest bastion containing the fort's gunpowder magazine. Fearing that an enormous explosion would result in mass casualties within the garrison, Olmstead made the weighty decision to surrender the fort. At around 2:30 p.m., Union soldiers, their artillery batteries located approximately one mile away on Tybee Island, witnessed the raising of a white sheet above Fort Pulaski. "On Tybee there was wild rejoicing. Men danced together on the beach, shook hands, and cheered General Gillmore as he rode along the line."[23]

Brigadier-General Quincy A. Gillmore at Charleston Harbor, 1863.
Harper's Weekly.

*Breaches in Fort Pulaski, April 1862, by Timothy
O'Sullivan. Library of Congress.*

If Olmstead had refused to surrender the fort,
a plan by Union leaders had been devised to take
Pulaski by direct assault. Within 24 hours, 10,000
Union soldiers could have been formed up and set
for the charge. Olmstead and his 385 officers and
men could not have withstood such an onslaught.
With Pulaski's walls breached in several locations,

a direct assault by such an overwhelming wave of combatants would have resulted in dire consequences for the defenders.

Flying a flag of truce, Captain Gillmore crossed the South Channel by boat and then approached the fort on foot accompanied by his aides. In a civil fashion, Colonel Olmstead greeted Gillmore and the two proceeded to the officers' quarters to work out the conditions of surrender. Each Confederate officer was forced to surrender his sword, while a mass formation was called and arms stacked in piles.

Both officers and enlisted would be taken as prisoners of war to various locations in New York State to be held. Some would eventually perish in captivity; others would be released in prisoner of war exchanges; while a few even swore allegiance to the Union. As the Rebels were being briefed on the terms of surrender that afternoon, Sergeant Abbott of the 48th New York witnessed the raising of the Union flag over Fort Pulaski: "The Old Flag of 76 was soon hoisted and its golden folds unfurled to the breeze and floated triumphant over the walls of the doomed fortress."[24]

The initial Federal occupation of Fort Pulaski was established by soldiers from several units including the 7th Connecticut Regiment, the 3rd Rhode Island Heavy Artillery, and a detachment of the New York Volunteer Engineers. "On June 1 the 7th Connecticut was relieved by the 48th New York, which remained on Cockspur until May 31, 1863."[25] The next six weeks of duty would be toilsome for the Federal troops garrisoned at Pulaski, with long and arduous work hours spent repairing the damages incurred during the bombardment.

Just two days following the surrender of Fort Pulaski, Major-General David Hunter would make his first in a series of contentious decisions without proper authority. Failing to notify his counterparts or superiors beforehand, Hunter declared all slaves on Cockspur Island free. A few weeks later Hunter issued one of the most controversial orders of the Civil War. General Order Number 11, issued on May 9, freed all slaves in the states of Georgia, Florida, and South Carolina. "The general's announcement caught most if not all Union commanders by surprise."[26] Hunter had sought neither congressional nor presidential approval prior to issuing the order, an unacceptable practice in a republic where civil authority reigns supreme.

These premature directives sent ripples in the Union organization, which had established its own timeline for freeing the slaves and facilitating this transition. After learning of Hunter's order, President Lincoln quickly took action. "On May 19, 1862, Lincoln declared Hunter's proclamation void and asserted that the president alone, not commanders in the field, had the authority to declare slaves free."[27]

Regardless of the legal technicalities and political ramifications, slaves who escaped to Cockspur or Hilton Head were free indeed. The Underground Railroad, which consisted of a series of safe houses, had been operating covertly for years throughout the South. The railroad's final destination which resulted in freedom for blacks had previously been north of the Mason-Dixon Line. With the Federals now occupying Southern islands, the terminus for freedom was often merely a rowboat's journey away.

Major-General Hunter was soon assisting abolitionists who were operating the Underground Railroad. He later worked with Harriet Tubman, the former slave and now abolitionist who had served as a "conductor" in this metaphorical railroad. Because Tubman had experience working with white abolitionists from the North, she was used as a liaison between the Union military and escaped slaves now serving as civilian scouts. She organized a small group of these men at the request of Union officers. "She found nine men, some of them riverboat pilots who knew every inch of the waterways threading through the coastal lowlands."[28] Hunter issued a pass to Tubman for travelling on Union transport ships along the coast. A memo signed by Hunter indicated the important role she played for the Union: "Harriet was sent to me from Boston by Governor Andrew, of Massachusetts, and is a valuable woman."[29]

Now with a commanding coastal presence in Port Royal Sound and the Savannah Harbor, Union strategists would shift their focus north and inland. Charleston Harbor, safeguarded by the sturdy and commanding Fort Sumter, was still firmly held by the Rebels. The cities of Charleston and Savannah were Confederate strongholds and were linked by a crucial railway that served as a main supply and logistical route. The vital Charleston and Savannah Railroad was no less than a lifeline for the Rebels stationed along the South Carolina and Georgia coasts.

Harriet Tubman, circa 1885. National Portrait Gallery.

Chapter III Source Notes

1. H. David Stone, *Vital Rails: The Charleston & Savannah Railroad and the Civil War in Coastal South Carolina* (Columbia, S.C.: University of South Carolina Press, 2008), 42.

2. *Confederate War Journal, Volume 2.* (New York and Lexington, KY: April, 1894), 51.

3. *Official Records of the Union and Confederate Navies. Series 1, Volume 12* (Washington, D.C.: Government Printing Office, 1894–1922), 263.

4. "The Day the Big Gun Shoot," *The State* newspaper (Columbia, S.C.: September 24, 2011).

5. John G. Abbott's Diary, November 7, 1861.

6. *Official Records of the Union and Confederate Navies. Series 1, Volume 12* (Washington, D.C.: Government Printing Office, 1894–1922), 262.

7. *Official Records of the Union and Confederate Navies. Series 1, Volume 12* (Washington, D.C.: Government Printing Office, 1894–1922), 263.

8. *Confederate War Journal, Volume 2* (New York and Lexington, KY: April, 1894), 51.

9. *Official Records of the Union and Confederate Navies. Series 1, Volume 12* (Washington, D.C.: Government Printing Office, 1894–1922), 261.

10. *Official Records of the Union and Confederate Armies. Series 1, Volume 6* (Washington, D.C.: Government Printing Office, 1894–1922), 312.

11. *A Guide to Historic Bluffton* (Bluffton, S.C.: The Bluffton Historical Preservation Society, Inc., 2007), 17.

12. John G. Abbott's Diary, November 10, 1861.

13. C. Vann Woodward, *Mary Chesnut's Civil War* (New Haven, CT: Yale, 1981), 232.

14. C. Vann Woodward, *Mary Chesnut's Civil War*

(New Haven, CT: Yale, 1981), 232.

15. Billie Burn, *An Island Named Daufuskie* (Spartanburg, S.C.: The Reprint Company, Publishers, 1991), 247.

16. Ralston B. Lattimore, Historical Handbook, Series No. 18 (Washington, D.C.: National Park Service, 1954), g.

17. Ralston B. Lattimore, *Historical Handbook, Series No. 18* (Washington, D.C.: National Park Service, 1954), h.

18. John G. Abbott's Diary, February 11, 1862.

19. Abraham J. Palmer, D.D., *The History of the Forty-Eighth Regiment, New York State Volunteers in the War of the Union 1861–1865* (Brooklyn, N.Y.: Veterans Association of the Regiment, 1885), 36.

20. Edward A. Miller, *Lincoln's Abolitionist General: The Biography of David Hunter* (Columbia, S.C.: University of South Carolina Press, 1997), viii.

21. Abraham J. Palmer, D.D., *The History of the Forty-Eighth Regiment, New York State Volunteers in the War of the Union 1861–1865* (Brooklyn, N.Y.: Veterans Association of the Regiment, 1885), 36.

22. John G. Abbott's Diary, April 11, 1862.

23. Ralston B. Lattimore, *Historical Handbook, Series No. 18* (Washington, D.C.: National Park Service, 1954), l.

24. John G. Abbott's Diary, April 11, 1862.

25. Ralston B. Lattimore, *Historical Handbook, Series No. 18* (Washington, D.C.: National Park Service, 1954), m.

26. Barbara Tomblin, *Bluejackets and Contrabands: African Americans and the Union Navy* (Lexington, KY: The University Press of Kentucky, 2009), 25.

27. Barbara Tomblin, *Bluejackets and Contrabands: African Americans and the Union Navy* (Lexington, KY: The University Press of Kentucky, 2009), 25.

28. "Intelligence in the Civil War," "Black Dispatches," Central Intelligence Agency https://www.cia.gov/library/publications/additional - publications/civil-war/p20.htm.

29. Sarah Bradford, *Harriet Tubman, The Moses of Her People* (Bedford, MA: Applewood Books, 1886), 140.

IV

The Confederate's Railroad

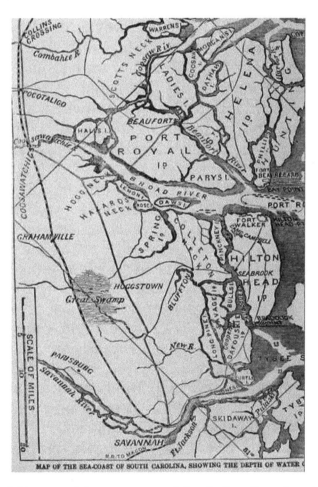

An 1861 map of the sea coast of South Carolina showing a segment of the Charleston and Savannah Railroad running from Savannah, GA, through Pocotaligo, S.C. Harper's Weekly.

By April of 1862, the Union's South Atlantic Blockading Squadron and the Department of the South had seized three critical forts overlooking two strategically important harbors, Port Royal and Savannah. The capture of Forts Walker, Beauregard, and Pulaski had given the Federals a commanding presence with vital operational bases and depots. Now occupying Hilton Head, Beaufort, and Cockspur Island, the Union military and its war planners were focusing heavily on the cities of Savannah and Charleston and the myriad important geographic features and other strategic points of interest along the coast. Approximately sixty miles of shoreline lay between these two cities, and of distinct significance to Northern commanders was the Charleston and Savannah Railroad.

The concept of a railway linking Charleston and Savannah had originated years before surveyors began mapping possible routes in 1854. The idea was largely spawned from a need to link Charleston to other rails in order to enhance the city's manufacturing and trade capabilities. Considering the impenetrable low- lying terrain that would need to be traversed, a construction project of this magnitude would amount to an enormous enterprise. "The building of the Charleston and Savannah Railroad was by far the largest single construction project and the largest industrial undertaking in the district."[1]

Several notable and influential planters from Bluffton and throughout the lowcountry were principal investors as well as directors of the railroad. Construction on the rail line would finally proceed in 1856 under railroad president, Thomas

F. Drayton, who would later serve as a brigadier-general in the Confederate army. Drayton owned a working plantation on Hilton Head and a summer home in Bluffton. Among the directors were William F. Colcock and Edmund Rhett, both men being associated with "The Bluffton Boys," calling for secession under the banner of The Bluffton Movement. Just prior to the outbreak of war, Colcock became the railroad's president.

During the planning stages, it was determined by Drayton and others that the cost of constructing the railroad would be more economical if slave labor was utilized. In many cases slaves were hired out to the Charleston and Savannah Railroad by their owners under detailed contracts that spelled out such specifics as clothing and medical care. The extensive and grueling manual labor required to clear the roadbeds through swamp, marsh, and woodlands was therefore conducted primarily by the hands of slaves. Living and working conditions along the construction route were unhealthy and exacting.

Nearly a year after construction began in 1856 the first tracks were being laid on the improved and graded road bed. The train began operating between the city of Charleston and the Savannah River in the spring of 1860. The last rails linking the two cities were finally laid in October of 1860 when the Savannah River crossing was completed. "At long last, on October 26, 1860, the final rail was laid on the track, and the last spike was driven to complete the connection between Charleston and the city of Savannah."[2]

On November 2, 1860, the official grand opening tour was completed when a train rolled down the track from Charleston to Savannah. The passenger cars contained many important persons and dignitaries on this trip, including Thomas F. Drayton and Charleston mayor Charles Macbeth.

This first exhibition jaunt was of particular historical significance and must have been monumental for those who had been part of the railroad and had witnessed its development from conception to completion. Future passengers would be in awe of the lowcountry's pristine natural splendor along the route. "From the train the countryside looked almost uninhabited, and passengers were struck by the natural beauty of the woods in the spring, when various shades of green and black decorated the rivers and swamps."[3]

The old road between Charleston and Savannah, which stretched for more than 100 miles, had taken days in a stagecoach or on horseback and included the inconvenience of ferry crossings. With the establishment of the new railroad, the voyage could now be traversed in relative comfort in a fraction of the time. Once regular service was established, the scenic trip between Charleston and Savannah took just nine hours, including brief stops at way stations.[4] The speed and convenience of traveling along this rail line would be of great consequence in upcoming Confederate troop movements during wartime operations.

Now in the spring of 1862, the railroad was playing a vital role for the Confederacy, which used the railway to shift limited troop assets to defend against amphibious incursions by Federal forces camped on the islands nearby.

General Robert E. Lee. Library of Congress.

On Hilton Head Island alone, approximately 13,000 Federal troops had swarmed on the beaches within days of the fall of Fort Walker. Now in 1862, the island's population reached 50,000 including soldiers, sailors, civilians, and freed slaves. A 1,300-foot pier was soon erected, which accommodated large ships and allowed for the offload of supplies and materials necessary to sustain the thriving Federal base and depot on Hilton Head.

Confederate infantry and cavalry units stationed in Bluffton were exceedingly conscious of the fact that a massive number of enemy troops were camped within rowing distance across the intercoastal waterway.[5] In the shadow of such a superior-size Union force, General Robert E. Lee considered the protection of the railroad of utmost importance. While serving as commander of the Department of South Carolina, Georgia, and Florida from his headquarters in Coosawhatchie, Lee's responsibility was to design and implement an overall defensive strategy along the coast.

After shoring up the defenses around Savannah and Charleston, Lee ordered obstacles to be placed in the rivers and creeks to impede federal gunboat incursions into the interior of the lowcountry. The clever general from Virginia then drafted an outline to protect the inland and the railroad itself by constructing a series of earthworks along the coast.[6] Many of these fortifications and lesser breastworks guarded routes which ran from potential amphibious landing sites. Lee also positioned cavalry units along the railroad's most vulnerable points to defend the line against assaults until reinforcements arrived via rail. This would also safeguard the railroad's use as an uninterrupted supply and logistics conduit and a tool to move and concentrate troops where the need arose. Travelling on horseback, Lee personally examined these construction efforts throughout the lowcountry. "Taking advantage of Federal inactivity [in the winter of 1861–62], he embarked on numerous trips to inspect the defenses along the coastline and personally direct much of the work."[7]

The value of the Charleston and Savannah Railroad was immeasurable to the Confederate army. The railroad was a lifeline for the Rebels, and Federal authorities immediately recognized its immense worth. Before General Thomas W. Sherman was replaced by Major-General Hunter in March of 1862 as commander of the Department of the South, he considered launching an amphibious-based assault against Bluffton, the New River Bridge earthworks, and Hardeeville. His ultimate target was the Savannah River railroad crossing. Sherman understood the significant step of gaining a foothold in Bluffton and Hardeeville in order to take control of the crossing. In a memo to fellow Union general Lorenzo Thomas, Sherman wrote: "an invasion of this sort would not only give us Savannah, but, if successful and strong enough to follow up the success, would shake the so-called Southern Confederacy to its very foundation."[8] Prior to initiating this offensive, however, Sherman was relieved of command.

The Union's initial success along the coast in 1861 and 1862 had been largely due to its overwhelming naval fire-power. Even the army's siege of Fort Pulaski was made possible when the

Rebels were forced to withdraw from Tybee Island because of its vulnerability from the sea. This enabled the Union army to establish batteries along Tybee's shoreline, which proved essential to the fort's reduction. The Southerners faced a daunting challenge when attempting to oppose Federal forces within range of their powerful naval artillery.

A sketch of the Charleston and Savannah Railroad, circa 1862.
Harper's Weekly.

Before marching against Charleston or Savannah, the Union would need to sever the Confederate railroad that linked these cities. Cutting the steel tracks would prevent the rapid deployment of Rebel reinforcements opposing such an invasion of either city. Reaching the railway, however, would present a new and diverse tactical challenge for the Yankees. These inland incursions along the rivers and creeks would place the Union army well out of range of their powerful warships. Small gunboats specifically outfitted for this type of mission would be required. Now in the spring of 1862, the Federals would need to conduct a more thorough reconnaissance of the South Carolina lowcountry before attempting a major assault on the Confederate's railroad.

Chapter IV Source Notes

1. Lawrence S. Rowland, Alexander Moore, and George C. Rogers, Jr., *The History of Beaufort County, South Carolina: Volume 1 1514–1861* (Columbia, S.C.: University of South Carolina Press, 1996), 392.

2. H. David Stone, *Vital Rails: The Charleston & Savannah Railroad and the Civil War in Coastal South Carolina* (Columbia, S.C.: University of South Carolina Press, 2008), 37.

3. H. David Stone, *Vital Rails: The Charleston & Savannah Railroad and the Civil War in Coastal South Carolina* (Columbia, S.C.: University of South Carolina Press, 2008), 33.

4. H. David Stone, *Vital Rails: The Charleston & Savannah Railroad and the Civil War in Coastal South Carolina* (Columbia, S.C.: University of South Carolina Press, 2008), 33.

5. Margaret Greer, *The Sands of Time. A History Of Hilton Head Island* (Hilton Head, S.C.: SouthArt, Inc., 1989), 44.

6. H. David Stone, *Vital Rails: The Charleston & Savannah Railroad and the Civil War in Coastal South Carolina* (Columbia, S.C.: University of South Carolina Press, 2008), 81–82.

7. H. David Stone, *Vital Rails: The Charleston & Savannah Railroad and the Civil War in Coastal*

South Carolina (Columbia, S.C.: University   of South Carolina Press, 2008), 73.

8. H. David Stone, *Vital Rails: The Charleston & Savannah Railroad and the Civil War in Coastal South Carolina* (Columbia, S.C.: University of South Carolina Press, 2008), 76.

V

Union Reconnaissance

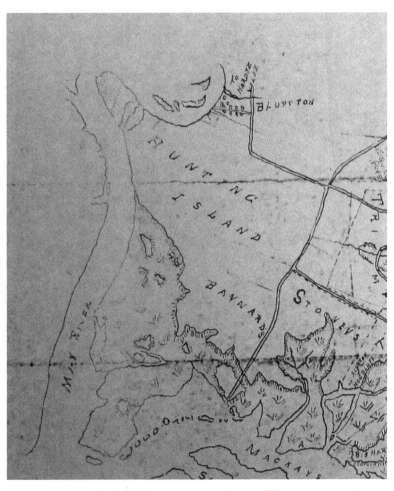

Antebellum map, courtesy of the
Bluffton Historical Preservation Society.

The Union's initial map reconnaissance of the lowcountry began in the early design stages by planners long before the South Atlantic Blockading Squadron set sail for Port Royal in late October of 1861. Maps of the region were studied for months prior to the squadron's final departure from Hampton Roads, Virginia. Shortly after the fall of Forts Walker and Beauregard on November 7, the Union began to physically reconnoiter the area. Intelligence gathering began by those involved in the various operations from the outset, as information was obtained from interviews with captured Confederates and former slaves. This information was sorted, deciphered, and then channeled upwards through the chain of command. Here it was reviewed and then disseminated to the officers who would be leading future missions.

A Civil War era–map of the region, including those used by the Union and Confederate militaries at the time, did not reveal the detail and complexity that actually exist on the earth's surface. Modern aerial images of the lowcountry disclose a much more intricate coastline with countless maritime navigational hazards in the form of sand bars, oyster beds, and more. Maps from the nineteenth century did, however, show most of the navigable rivers. In the greater Bluffton area these include the Broad, Chechessee, Colleton, Okatie, May, and New Rivers.

The Union's ultimate objectives of Savannah and Charleston and the railroad linking these cities were the central focus of Federal strategists based on Hilton Head. Regardless of the lesser operations being carried out throughout the lowcountry at any given time, these two major cities and the lifeline connecting them remained in the peripheral vision of Northern commanders at all times.

The railroad makes a wide-arching curve inland around the natural obstacles of the rivers and creeks that protrude into the interior. As the rail line ran through Grahamville, Coosawhatchie, and Pocotaligo Station, its geographic location provided the Union with several vulnerable points of interest. These were places where the rivers and creeks jutted further inland, allowing Union commanders stationed on Hilton Head and Fort Pulaski to insert troops nearer to the railroad, while their smaller gunboats provided cover.

Landing troops upstream on the banks of the May River in an effort to attack the railway at Hardeeville, however, would require a march of approximately 16 miles. Pushing riverboats upstream along the New River would potentially enable the Federals to make landfall nearer to Hardeeville, but with a greater risk from Confederate-placed obstacles along the river, as well as gun batteries positioned at Red Bluff.

At the time the Union was conducting siege operations on the Confederate-held Fort Pulaski in March of 1862, they were simultaneously beginning a more aggressive reconnaissance of the inland waterways between Savannah and Charleston. The Federals conducted reconnaissance-in-force operations in an effort to probe Rebel defenses and gain intelligence on the enemy's positions, strengths, weaknesses, and reactions.

Even with thousands of Federal troops camped within rowing distance across the intercoastal waterway, the town of Bluffton had remained relatively quiet since the Union victory at Port Royal in November of 1861. This would change in March of 1862, when the Union began conducting reconnaissance-in-force incursions along the May River.

On March 25, from his headquarters on Hilton Head Island, Lieutenant-Colonel John H. Jackson of the 3rd New Hampshire Volunteers submitted a detailed report to his superior, Colonel Enoch Q. Fellows. Jackson's account of a reconnaissance-in-force along the May River lasting several days included the following: "Sir: I have the honor to report that, in compliance with Special Orders, No. 67, March 18, 1862, I proceeded on the 19th, with 24 officers and [several hundred] enlisted men, on a reconnaissance in force on May River, running between the Islands of Bull and Savage and the main-land."[1]

The newly constructed Union pier on Hilton Head Island, April 1862. Library of Congress.

Colonel Jackson noted that 16 small boats were employed in the operation, including three that carried artillery pieces in support of the landing parties.

After an evening rain delay on Wednesday, March 19, Jackson and his men embarked from Hilton Head Island at 2:30 a.m. on Thursday, March 20. Lieutenant-Colonel Jackson first ordered two companies in several boats under the command of Captain Randlett to proceed to Buckingham Ferry. With the remainder of the party, Jackson continued up the May River, "...and about daybreak landed on a hard beach at Dr. James Kirk's plantation [Hunting Island Plantation], on the main-land, and one mile from Bluffton."[2]

This 946-acre plantation, which roughly encompassed today's Alljoy community, was a subdivision of the original Devil's Elbow Barony. Several nineteenth-century maps indicate that a sizeable building was located within a ¼-mile radius of Alljoy Landing. This and other evidence suggests that the structure was possibly Hunting Island Plantation's primary dwelling.

Despite its name, and contrary to the writings of several officers who were unfamiliar with Bluffton during the war, Hunting Island Plantation, not to be confused with Hunting Island near St. Helena, was not an island, but was part of the Bluffton mainland. Through the years, the term "Plantation" was erroneously omitted from some maps and writings. In the course of time, and with the absence of a few select old maps that revealed its true location, this inaccuracy was often repeated. As a result, researchers and writers later attempting to pinpoint "Hunting Island" with written records alone often found themselves searching for an actual island.

Meanwhile, as Lieutenant-Colonel Jackson and his troops from the 3rd New Hampshire approached Hunting Island Plantation, they spotted a group of Confederate cavalry skirting the adjacent wood line. Jackson ordered his artillerymen to shell the area, forcing the Rebel troopers to gallop beyond the cannon's range. He then sent a party of skirmishers ashore led by Captain Plimpton in the direction of Buckingham Ferry, "to assist Captain Randlett, and to ascertain what other pickets [lookouts] there were near there, and, if possible, to capture them."[3]

During the Civil War the term skirmisher typically referred to a smaller group of infantry, dismounted cavalry, or scouts, which had a greater ability to maneuver and monitor the enemy's movements. As a result, Plimpton and his band of skirmishers encircled four Confederate lookouts stationed at Buckingham Ferry, trapping them against Mackay Creek. The Rebels were consequently prevented from utilizing their only escape route, which ran west along Fording Island Road.

Because of the important role that the lookouts played in monitoring Federal movements along the inland waterways surrounding Bluffton, the capture of the Confederates at Buckingham Ferry was noteworthy. The incident would continually remind future Confederate troopers of their vulnerability while on this and other picket posts surrounding the greater Bluffton peninsula.

After being captured, the four Rebels were disarmed of "their rifles and long knives"[4] and sent in boats to Hilton Head to be detained and questioned. Captain Randlett and the other parties then boarded their crafts at Buckingham Ferry and returned to the May River. Jackson's 3rd New Hampshire rowed to Bull Island, which is positioned across the May River from Hunting Island Plantation, and camped there for the night.

On the next morning, Friday, March 21, Jackson's force boarded their vessels and crossed Bull Creek to the Savage Islands after receiving intelligence indicating that Rebel lookouts were stationed there. After thoroughly combing the islands and finding no Rebels, they returned to their makeshift camp on Bull Island for the second night.

Bright and early on the morning of Saturday, March 22, the Yankees embarked once again and crossed the May River, landing at Hunting Island Plantation on the mainland. As outlined, the plan of the day called for Jackson's 3rd New Hampshire to conduct a reconnaissance-in-force throughout the town of Bluffton in order to gather pertinent intelligence on Confederate troop strength, and to determine the presence or nonexistence of earthworks or fortifications on the mainland.

Reports of the Union landing were soon filtering in to Major John B. Willcoxon, Cavalry Commander of the Phillips Legion stationed at Bluffton, who immediately forwarded these dispatches to Brigadier-General Thomas F. Drayton in Hardeeville. The urgent messages indicated that Union soldiers "were advancing on

Bluffton in two columns, one column by the gate and one around by the beach or bluff."[5]

Just as Confederate reports had indicated, Lieutenant-Colonel Jackson's companies had begun marching in columns towards Bluffton from Hunting Island Plantation at a hurried pace. As the troops of the 3rd New Hampshire advanced into the town from the east, Rebel skirmishers were lying in wait. Musket fire erupted as Jackson's lead elements exchanged shots with the gray-clad soldiers. The larger Union force compelled the outnumbered Rebels to pull back west along River Road, occasionally referred to as Hardeeville Road during the war, and currently known as May River Road. Jackson later wrote: "We arrived at Bluffton at 12:00 p.m., driving the pickets through the town and a short distance beyond, but finding it impossible to cut them off, abandoned the pursuit."[6] As the Confederates halted and hunkered down in fighting positions just west of the town, the men of the 3rd New Hampshire ended the chase and began a quick search of Bluffton.

Other than scouring through several buildings in a quest to locate military-related items, no damage was reportedly inflicted by the Union army. After the hasty search, Jackson marched his now fatigued men back to Hunting Island Plantation, where they boarded boats and once again crossed the May River to camp in relative safety on Bull Island for the third night.

Major-General John C. Pemberton had recently assumed command of the Department of South Carolina, Georgia, and Florida on March 4, 1862. Pemberton replaced the able Robert E.

Lee, who had been ordered to Richmond, to assume command of the Army of Northern Virginia. After being informed of the initial Union landing at Hunting Island Plantation on Thursday, March 20, Pemberton had directed Brigadier-General Drayton, commander of the Sixth Military District of South Carolina, to use all available forces and bear down on Jackson's regiment. "I consider that there is a sufficient number of troops now in hand and near Bluffton to capture or drive the enemy from his position at Hunting Island [Plantation]. This you will endeavor to do, if not already done, on the receipt of this communication."[7]

Having completed their reconnaissance of Bluffton, Jackson's 3rd New Hampshire spent Sunday foraging for food and supplies on Bull Island. Foraging was a vital and indispensable activity for the thousands of Federal troops based on Hilton Head, who had only limited supplies and materials available on the island. The surrounding islands such as Bull and Callawassie had been abandoned by local land owners and offered a plethora of useful articles in addition to food such as wild game and livestock. "They [Union soldiers] desperately needed building materials of all kinds, i.e., windows, doors, frames, anything of use. Prior to the war Hilton Head was a remote place, home to perhaps a few hundred people. Wartime, Union Hilton Head occasionally reached 50,000 occupants—soldiers and civilians, and all manner of new buildings were needed."[8] After bivouacking on Bull Island for the fourth and final night, Jackson's 3rd New

Hampshire returned to Hilton Head the next morning, concluding their protracted mission.

Jackson's well thought out plan to encircle and capture the Rebel lookouts posted at Buckingham Ferry proved effective, and combined with a productive reconnaissance, resulted in an overall successful Union mission. After the operation was complete four Rebel pickets had been captured and valuable intelligence concerning the enemy gathered. The Confederates also suffered two horses wounded by musket fire during the resultant skirmish.

Perhaps of more worth and likely for the first time during the conflict, Northern soldiers had witnessed the affluent, but now war-torn village of Bluffton. As a New York soldier later described the scene, "But the houses were desolate and given up to pillage, the happy households scattered..."9 The abandoned homes belonged to some of the wealthiest and most influential men from throughout the lowcountry. This list included many high-ranking officers such as Brigadier-General Drayton, Colonel Joseph J. Stoney, Colonel Ephraim Mikell Seabrook, Captain M.J. Kirk, Captain Middleton Stuart, and many others. The disproportionately high number of officer's residences within Bluffton's one square mile would have been equivalent to an officer's housing section of a modern base, providing a plethora of intelligence for their adversaries.

From a tactical standpoint, Lieutenant-Colonel Jackson had gained valuable data during the mission. According to official reports, he learned that the town contained no earthworks or strongholds. In addition, "the nearest approach to artillery was an old dismounted iron gun on the bluff near the church and on the bank of the river."[10] Records also indicate that the nearest earthworks were located at the strategically important New River Bridge west of Pritchardville. A small battery was situated just west of the river, overlooking this valuable crossing, and was manned by members of the Beaufort Artillery, along with Company C from the 11th South Carolina Infantry.[11]

Jackson found no civilians residing in the town with the exception of three black men, who provided the Federals with information. Both Union and Confederate military accounts on separate occasions describe these particular individuals as living independently and moving freely within the town of Bluffton.[12] Official reports indicate that they were questioned by both Northern and Southern troops at separate junctures and were allowed to resume their activities.

Although a few slaves and free blacks chose to remain on their respective estates, most began fleeing to Hilton Head soon after the Union victory at Port Royal in November of 1861. In small groups of various sizes, the runaways absconded in rowboats to Hilton Head from nearby plantations on Pinckney and St. Helena Islands and the mainland. Northern officials quickly established a refugee camp on Hilton Head, providing housing, blankets, and meals for the former slaves. By February of 1862, the site accommodated 600 freedmen according to the testimony of Federal officials.[13]

Throughout the spring of 1862, the North continued to probe the winding rivers and creeks throughout the lowcountry. A noteworthy reconnaissance-in-force operation was carried out by the Federals on May 29. General Isaac Stevens had directed Colonel Benjamin C. Christ to lead an expedition with the objective of severing the Charleston and Savannah Railroad at Pocotaligo. In addition to cutting the rail line, leaders would gather valuable intelligence on Rebel bulwarks and troop positions.

The 50th Pennsylvania Volunteers would be the primary regiment conducting the offensive, with detachments from several other key units in support. After departing Beaufort late in the evening on May 28, the Union force steamed up the Broad River in transports early the next morning. Once across Port Royal Ferry, the Yankees landed and marched past Gardens Corner, then continued along Sheldon Church Road.[14] After receiving sporadic and harassing fire from Confederate pickets and skirmishers aligned along the route, the Yankees finally reached the causeway east of Old Pocotaligo. The crossing was being observed by several Rebel cavalry units including the 1st Battalion, South Carolina Cavalry led by Major Joseph H. Morgan and the Rutledge Mounted Riflemen commanded by Captain William L. Trenholm. Once the Union's progress towards the railroad was stymied near the Pocotaligo River by the frequent assaults of Southern troops, Colonel Christ was forced to pull his physically drained men back and retire to Port Royal Ferry.

Freed slaves planting sweet potatoes, circa 1862.
Library of Congress.

At the conclusion of the prolonged engagement, each adversary had suffered two killed and several wounded. "General Stevens considered the operation another successful reconnaissance mission."[15] Stevens' assessment was a matter of opinion, however, as the Confederates viewed the outcome otherwise. Under the command of Colonel William S. Walker, the Rebels had reacted well to the Union offensive. The Southern leadership was particularly successful in utilizing the Charleston and Savannah Railroad to shift troop strength to the threatened area. Ultimately, the much desired "Confederate Railroad" remained unscathed.

In the meantime, decisive battles were occurring in other states to the west and north. General Ulysses S. Grant pulled off a crucial victory in early April at the Battle of Shiloh in Tennessee. Although Grant had been surrounded by Confederate forces and corralled in a perilous circumstance, Northern reinforcements arrived in the closing moments to alter the engagement's outcome.

Several more key battles occurred in the late spring and early summer of 1862, when McClellan's Army of the Potomac drove towards the core of the South. "Hard fighting brought the Union army to within four miles of Richmond, the heart and symbol of the Confederacy."[16] McClellan soon learned, however, that Rebel forces were rapidly closing in on the capitol at Washington. After a series of battles known as "The Seven Days," General Robert E. Lee, formerly in command at Coosawhatchie, defeated McClellan and thus perpetuated the duration of the war.

Closer to home in the Battle of Secessionville just south of Charleston, Union Brigadier-General Henry Benham attempted an aggressive frontal assault on Fort Lamar in June. The Confederates effectively repelled the attack and defeated the Federals, who suffered over 600 casualties to the Rebels' estimated 200. Later the same month, Northern forces of the 55th Pennsylvania landed at Simmons Bluff south of Charleston, their principal aim being to drive inland and destroy a section of the Charleston and Savannah Railroad. Despite routing a startled encampment of the 16th South Carolina Infantry, the Yankees returned to their ships and abandoned their plans to cut the railroad.[17]

In the interim, the 48th New York had been in garrison at Fort Pulaski since May 25, 1862. With few exceptions, the majority of the regiment's stint at the fort consisted of picket and guard duties, monotonous marching drills, and the always unpopular fatigue duty. A steamship made regular passages to Hilton Head Island several days per week, providing mail, supplies, materials, and foodstuffs to the garrison on Cockspur Island. On most Sundays at 4:00 p.m. the soldiers would congregate for their regular weekly church service. Occasionally companies or individual squads would be chosen to go on routine river patrols aboard various gunboats.[18] By this time communications had been established between Fort Pulaski and Braddock's Point on the South end of Hilton Head. First, signal stations were built and later a submerged telegraph cable spanning roughly five miles was laid between the sites.[19]

Living conditions for soldiers during the Civil War were harsh and unsanitary. Death from disease and illness was common for both Union and Confederate soldiers, who often succumbed to such sicknesses as dysentery, malaria, and pneumonia. Medical practices during the war were rudimentary, and supplies, especially for the South, were limited and inadequate. Many otherwise avertable deaths resulted from a lack of modern medical techniques and drugs.

Although there were likely more, Sergeant Abbott mentions seven burials in his diary from May through September while at Fort Pulaski.[20] One of these deaths amounted to a critical loss for Abbott's regiment, the 48th New York. On the afternoon of June 18, Colonel James H. Perry, the regiment's commander, fell unconscious and died suddenly while in his quarters at the fort.[21] Private Abraham J. Palmer listed Perry's death as apoplexy, a term often used in the 1800s to describe not only cerebral apoplexy, or stroke, but other deaths preceded by sudden unconsciousness as well. "His death will be greatly felt by all," Abbott penned in his diary.[22] After Perry's unforeseen death, Lieutenant-Colonel William Barton was promoted to Colonel as Perry's successor.

Back at the Rebel base camp in Bluffton, Captain John H. Mickler had replaced Captain Middleton Stuart as commander of Company E, 11th South Carolina Infantry. Formerly enlisted as a sergeant, Mickler had received a field commission as a result of his effectiveness as a daring and capable scout. He was subsequently elected by his peers to command Company E under the South Carolina militia election system.[23]

Mickler was now planning a surprise attack on the Yankees, who had boldly marched into Bluffton and skirmished with the Rebels a few months earlier. While covertly reconnoitering the waters around Pinckney Island, Captain Mickler had discovered a way to approach a Union campsite on the island undetected. Company H of Lieutenant-Colonel John H. Jackson's 3rd New Hampshire Volunteers was posted on Pinckney Island. The Company was stationed at the site of a plantation house referred to as The Point,[24] with pickets positioned along the western shoreline to observe the Confederate-held mainland across Mackay Creek.

From Bear Island, situated adjacent to present-day Colleton River Plantation, Mickler and Captain Stephen Elliott launched the mission at 3:00 a.m. on August 21, 1862. With six rowboats and a total of 120 men, the raiders crossed Mackay Creek and landed on Pinckney Island just prior to dawn.[25] The Confederates silently approached the area undetected and surrounded the Federal campsite. When the Southerners demanded surrender a close-quarters skirmish erupted. Elliott later reported that 15 of the enemy were killed and 4 wounded in the ensuing melee. The Rebels subsequently captured 36 members of the 3rd New Hampshire and swiftly departed with the prisoners in rowboats. Six of the Federals were fortunate enough to escape unharmed.

Elliott and Mickler would receive considerable accolades for the Pinckney Island raid. Mickler's actions were commended by Colonel William S. Walker on August 22 in a letter to the adjutant general: "Captain Mickler has but recently been under my command, but in that short time his boldness as a scout and his gallantry as a leader have sustained his well-earned reputation." On August 27 the two young officers were praised for their "gallantry" by Major-General John C. Pemberton, who expressed his utmost approval of their deeds.[26]

On September 30, 1862, just over one month after Captain Mickler's lethal raid on Pinckney Island, the North answered with a strike along the May River. This and the next two expeditions into Bluffton were conducted primarily by the 48th New York. Abraham J. Palmer explained that on September 30, the 48th Regiment steamed up the May River and destroyed a vast saltworks production facility west of the town. Palmer even confessed the regiment's role in plundering some of Bluffton's stately homes during the mission. These acts included "'confiscating' a piano and such furniture as could be brought away for the officers' quarters in the fort [Pulaski]."[27]

In addition to Palmer's report of the September 30 expedition, there also exists a dispatch detailing the action written by Colonel William Barton, the regiment's recently promoted commander.[28] From his Fort Pulaski headquarters, Barton briefed Lieutenant-Colonel Prentice, Assistant Adjutant General, clarifying that the objective of the mission was to surprise the Confederates bivouacked in the town and subsequently destroy a saltworks factory located on a plantation upstream from the village.

The plan's design called for offloading the troops 1 ½ miles downstream from Bluffton on the banks of Hunting Island Plantation.

Colonel, and later, General William B. Barton,
circa 1861. Library of Congress.

Barton's force would then encircle the town
and block the Rebels' westerly escape route along
present-day May River Road. Just before daylight,

however, these plans went awry as the ships approached the landing site. The steamer *Planter* that was carrying the Federal troops ran aground amid thick fog within ½-mile of the proposed landing site. Confederate lookouts posted on Hunting Island Plantation near present-day Alljoy Landing spotted the vessels and notified the cavalry commander of outposts in Bluffton.

The *Planter* was the former Confederate States armed transport craft that had been daringly steered out of Charleston Harbor past the Confederate guns of Fort Sumter under the cover of darkness in May of 1862. Once reaching the Federal blockade ships in the Atlantic, the *Planter's* pilot, a slave named Robert Smalls, presented the captured prize to Union navy officials. Among the passengers on board the night of the escape from Charleston Harbor were a number of men, women, and children slaves who now celebrated their freedom as a result. Smalls was highly commended for his actions by Rear Admiral Samuel F. DuPont, who consequently employed Smalls as a civilian pilot and later a captain due to his familiarity with the coastal waters of the lowcounty.[29]

In the meantime, as soon as the *Planter* was dislodged and afloat, Colonel Barton landed several companies of the regiment on Hunting Island Plantation. As the stretching columns of blue began marching towards Bluffton, the supporting steamships remained abreast and slightly ahead of the soldiers on their far left flank. "The gunboats kept just ahead of the infantry and kept shelling the woods ahead of them until they arrived in Bluffton," recalled John G. Abbott of the 48th New York.[30]

Robert Smalls, circa 1862. Library of Congress.

The armed transport Planter, circa 1862. Library of Congress.

Once the head of the long Yankee columns entered Bluffton, the large element continued filing west through the town along May River Road in the direction of Crowell's Plantation situated on the banks of the May River. Providing cover fire, the steamships continued upstream just forward of the dismounted soldiers. From his armed transport, Colonel Barton then observed several Rebel companies of cavalry and a company of infantry staged west of the town. The gunboats then engaged this group of "200 cavalry and a body of infantry" with mounted artillery.[31]

As the dismounted soldiers of the 48th New York trekked west beyond Bluffton, they came upon this same contingent of Rebels, who had now taken up fighting positions in an effort to slow the Yankee advance. "At first the Rebels made a stand in line of battle on the Old Turnpike [May River Road] to receive our infantry, but the gunboats again put them to flight."[32]

Crowell's Plantation contained an extensive salt production plant. These facilities were essential for the South during the war. "It was considered so important that Confederate President Jefferson Davis would issue an order that relieved men who were involved in the coastal production of the substance from military service."[33] Prior to refrigeration, salt was used to preserve meats, fish, and many other food products. Its use also extended to curing leather during the tanning process. The production and distribution of salt was of such marked importance and necessity to the armies of both North and South that missions were often carried out exclusively to destroy enemy facilities.

After demolishing the plant's components at Crowell's Plantation, which consisted of furnaces, vats, and kettles, the 48th New York then discovered another factory nearby that was even more wide-ranging. According to Colonel Barton, "These last were very extensive, the vats extending for more than a quarter of a mile."[34] Having accomplished the mission's primary objective of destroying the saltworks, Barton's dismounted elements boarded the transports after a strenuous day and rested along the scenic lowcountry passage to Fort Pulaski. Colonel Barton's 48th Regiment suffered no fatalities during the skirmish and Rebel casualty reports for the engagement were unavailable.

Also in September of 1862, a significant change of command occurred within the Confederate army in the lowcountry. Control of the Department of South Carolina, Georgia, and Florida, was transferred from General Pemberton to the leadership of General P.G.T Beauregard.

While the Union's Department of the South continued its activities along the southeastern coast, major battles were being waged further north in other theatres of the war. In September, Lee and McClellan met at a place known as Antietam Creek in one of the goriest matches of the conflict. As this victory went to the Union, the North's far-reaching scheme was becoming apparent. "Now after more than a year of hostilities, the grand strategy of the North began to emerge; a total blockade on the sea, and the splitting of the Confederacy by way of the western rivers."35 Despite moderate success in maintaining a firm footing along the South Carolina coast, the Rebels were gradually losing ground in the overall struggle.

In the fall of 1862, the 48th New York continued to venture from their nest at Fort Pulaski, conducting river patrols and reconnaissance operations throughout the lowcountry. On the regiment's second significant incursion, which took place on October 18, they once again made the twisting maritime passage to Bluffton. The purpose of this exploit was to extract two former slaves who had been conducting a spy mission in Bluffton. Union commanders had previously recognized an opportunity to surreptitiously insert black scouts onto the mainland who were residing at refugee camps on Hilton Head and Cockspur Islands. Because many slaves were still occupying their owner's property, these spies could in some cases gather intelligence without drawing suspicion from Rebel soldiers. According to Sergeant Abbott, these "spies" had been planted on the Bluffton mainland in the late-night hours of October 12.[36] Now on October 18, Colonel Barton along with Company B of the 48th New York departed Fort Pulaski at 9:00 a.m. to extract the two spies. Barton successfully rendezvoused with the infiltrators upriver from the town near the saltworks facilities which had been destroyed on September 30. The colonel then directed the pilot of the *Planter*, likely Robert Smalls, whom years later became a prominent United States Congressman, to return to Fort Pulaski.[37]

As the Federals steamed downstream along the May River, Confederate soldiers were cunningly lying in wait in a concealed position high atop the bluffs near the town. Sergeant Abbott made the following diary entry that evening: "When about from the town they was fired unto by some rebel infantry which was concealed in the woods. There was about 100 of them."[38]

The Rebels' piercing barrage of musket fire struck four soldiers aboard the *Planter*. Colonel Barton then ordered his artillerymen onboard the steamer to return fire. "We killed some of them and threw the grape and canister [artillery shells filled with shot] amongst them, when they skedaddled..."[39] After the pouncing ambush and subsequent short-lived bout, the *Planter* hurried the wounded to Fort Pulaski. Union Corporal George Durand of Company B, who was struck in the torrent of fire, succumbed to his injuries and died the following day. As Private Abraham J. Palmer recalled, "He was the first man of the regiment to fall at the hands of the enemy."[40]

After just one month as commander of the Department of South Carolina, Georgia, and Florida, General Beauregard received an intelligence dispatch suggesting an intended Union attack on the Charleston and Savannah Railroad. Beauregard's sources proved trustworthy. On the evening of October 21, a large element totaling 4,448 men commanded by Brigadier-General J.M. Brannan boarded steamships and departed Hilton Head Island.[41]

By the early morning hours of October 22, the Federals had cruised up the Broad River and landed a force at Mackey's Point. The regiments then quickly marched north along Mackey's Point Road in an effort to reach and destroy the railroad at Pocotaligo, then cut the telegraph wire running contiguous with the tracks. As Brannan's leading elements advanced along the route, they were engaged at a creek crossing by Confederate artillerymen from positions at Caston's Plantation. The Rebels then pulled back. This engagement cycle directed by Rebel commanders was repeated at Frampton Plantation. The Confederates destroyed small bridges along the route as they withdrew, further hampering the Union advance.

As General Brannan slowly but obstinately fought his way north along Mackey's Point Road on the morning of October 22, the 48th New York had continued steaming further up the Broad River until it transitioned into the Coosawhatchie River. Barton's regiment landed within two miles of Coosawhatchie and swiftly proceeded northwest along the main road into the town. As the outnumbered Rebels struggled to slow Brannan's progress towards Pocotaligo, General Beauregard and Colonel William S. Walker ordered reinforcements from Hardeeville via the Charleston and Savannah Railroad to proceed to Pocotaligo.

ARMY SIGNAL TELEGRAPH.

From The History of the Forty-Eighth Regiment

In the interim, the 48th New York reached Coosawhatchie and finally espied the much sought-after Confederate railroad. While standing alongside the vital artery linking the Southern strongholds of Charleston and Savannah, they heard the unmistakable sound of a locomotive's whistle. As one of the trains carrying Confederate reinforcements from Hardeeville approached Coosawhatchie, Colonel Barton's 48th New York ambushed the stunned Rebels, delivering a lethal burst of musket and artillery fire at the passing cars.

The hasty ambuscade killed several Rebels and wounded others. Barton then directed his men to cut the steel tracks in several places and sever the neighboring telegraph wire. In his diary entry Sergeant Abbott noted: "We fired into it [train] and killed several and many jumped off and skedaddled. We then rushed on to the track, tore it up and cut the telegraph wires."[42]

General Brannan was now meeting with heavy resistance as he attempted to reach and sever the railroad at Pocotaligo. Once his lead skirmishers arrived at the Pocotaligo Bridge, which had been wiped out by the Rebels, Brannan was forced to withdraw his regiments and return south along Mackey's Point Road after suffering substantial losses. In a report to his adjutant-general, Brannan wrote: "I deemed it expedient to move on Mackey's Point, which I did in successive lines of defense, burying my dead and carrying our wounded with us on such stretchers as we could manufacture from branches of trees, blankets, etc., and received no molestation from the Rebels; embarked and returned to Hilton Head on the 23rd instant."[43]

After promptly dismantling a section of the rail line at Coosawhatchie, Colonel Barton then withdrew the regiment back to the waiting gunboats, skirmishing with a revengeful and pesky Confederate cavalry as they moved. The 48th managed to board the transports safely, however, and then returned to Hilton Head and later to Fort Pulaski.

Although one train had been ambushed while rushing Confederates to the battle, others enabled reinforcements to be effectively placed in order to stymie the Union advance on Pocotaligo. Notwithstanding the effectiveness of the 48th New York at Coosawhatchie, the overall mission did not bode well for future Yankee endeavors to destroy the prized Charleston and Savannah Railroad. The North's offensive was plainly foiled by a lesser Rebel force. In the day long Second Battle of Pocotaligo, the Federals suffered 337 casualties. The Confederates' killed, wounded, or missing, equaled relatively less at 163.

Colonel William S. Walker and General P.G.T Beauregard had successfully shifted reinforcements along the Charleston and Savannah Railroad. Brigadier-General Thomas F. Drayton's earlier prophecy of the railroad's prospective military value had come to fruition: "This much neglected railway will be the cheapest and most formidable earthwork that could have been devised to give confidence and security at home and repel invasion from abroad."44

While General Beauregard's military department was tenaciously defending the lowcountry coastline against inland incursions by the Union's Department of the South, a monumental proclamation was read by President Lincoln. On

January 1, 1863, Lincoln issued the Emancipation Proclamation, declaring all slaves free. "I do order and declare that all persons held as slaves within said designated States, and parts of States, are, and henceforward shall be free; and that the Executive government of the United States, including the military and naval authorities thereof, will recognize and maintain the freedom of said persons."[45]

Upon hearing the words of this historic and spiritually uplifting decree, former slaves on Hilton Head, Beaufort, and Cockspur Island jubilantly celebrated their glorious freedom so long awaited. This precious and cherished gift had been courtesy of the selfless sacrifices of the boys in blue. Although the declaration was a great moral victory, to blacks still in bondage it was a bittersweet announcement that only heightened their anxiousness and desire for liberty.

As the New Year of 1863 rang in, Captain Mickler and his intrepid band of scouts camped in Bluffton continued their string of nocturnal raids and captures behind enemy lines. Even with far superior numbers and isolated on an island, the Yankees were soberly reminded of their vulnerability once again. In January, four of Mickler's capable scouts quietly slipped across Calibogue Sound in a small craft to execute a daring nighttime operation; capturing Private Caleb Jones of the 9th Maine Infantry near his camp at Spanish Wells on Hilton Head.[46] As a result, valuable intelligence was obtained from Jones concerning the operations of Union signal towers and observatories.

The signal towers were linked in a series, which enabled signal personnel to maintain rapid communications through the use of flags during the day and lanterns at night. Generals Beauregard and Walker consequently formulated a plot to seize the signal codebook from one of the towers on Hilton Head, which would theoretically enable the Confederates to decipher Union communications.

The newly promoted General Walker predictably chose Captain Mickler to carry out this risky assignment. On the evening of March 12, 1863, Mickler and 25 men from Company E embarked in rowboats from the Bluffton mainland. The team made landfall at the base of the steep bluffs along Spanish Wells at around midnight. Mickler and his raiders quietly ascended the embankment and stalked the soldiers who had been assigned night watch at the selected tower. Mickler's men captured nine soldiers from the 9th Maine Infantry who were guarding and manning the signal tower. The Rebels then seized the treasured codebook that Generals Beauregard and Walker had so eagerly sought. Slipping away in their rowboats with the bound Yankee prisoners, the obscure Confederates headed for the mouth of the May River, their silhouettes gradually fading in the night.

On the evening of Mickler's foray, Sergeant Abbott of the 48th New York was on Hilton Head after being granted a routine liberty pass to leave Fort Pulaski for several days. At 1:00 a.m., Abbott heard the alarms echo throughout the numerous camps of the island. The loud drums sounded the rousing call to arms. "At 1 o'clock at night The Long Roll Beat and the regiment was soon off to Spanish Wells where 20 Rebels had landed and captured our pickets and some of the signal corps."[47] By the time the Federal reaction forces arrived, however, Mickler and his stealthy band of scouts had crossed Calibogue Sound and vanished. The Rebels were soon within Confederate-held territory, arriving safely on the Bluffton mainland. The detainees were then transported to Hardeeville and transferred to Southern officials, where the valuable codebook along with information obtained from questioning was later used to the Confederates' advantage.

Mickler and his company continued to garner high praise throughout the lowcountry from allied officers and civilian authorities alike. For his actions, he was later honored with an inscribed sword. The handsome weapon, which was specially ordered from London, was presented to the daring captain by Lieutenant-Colonel Stokes of the 4th South Carolina Cavalry and several other officers.[48]

The successful exploits and guerrilla-style tactics employed by Captain Mickler and the adept men of Company E had also drawn the attention of Union commanders within the Department of the South. A sweeping and destructive Northern offensive was soon forthcoming, but as a byproduct of regional policy objectives beyond Mickler's influence.

Chapter V Source Notes

1. *Official Records of the Union and Confederate Armies, Series 1, Volume 6* (Washington, D.C.: Government Printing Office, 1894–1922), 101.

2. *Official Records of the Union and Confederate Armies, Series 1, Volume 6* (Washington, D.C.: Government Printing Office, 1894–1922), 101.

3. *Official Records of the Union and Confederate Armies, Series 1, Volume 6* (Washington, D.C.: Government Printing Office, 1894–1922), 101.

4. *Official Records of the Union and Confederate Armies. Series 1, Volume 6.* (Washington, D.C.: Government Printing Office, 1894–1922), 102.

5. *Official Records of the Union and Confederate Armies, Series 1, Volume 6* (Washington, D.C.: Government Printing Office, 1894–1922), 105.

6. *Official Records of the Union and Confederate Armies, Series 1, Volume 6* (Washington, D.C.: Government Printing Office, 1894–1922), 102.

7. *Official Records of the Union and Confederate Armies, Series 1, Volume 6* (Washington, D.C.: Government Printing Office, 1894–1922), 110.

8. William A. Behan, *A Short History of Callawassie Island, South Carolina. The Lives and Times of Its Owners and Residents, 1711–1985.* (Lincoln, NE: iUniverse, 2004), 79.

9. James M. Nichols, *Perry's Saints; or The Fighting Parsons Regiment in the War of the Rebellion* (Boston, MA: D. Lothrop and Company, 1886), 123.

10. *Official Records of the Union and Confederate Armies, Series 1, Volume 6* (Washington, D.C.: Government Printing Office, 1894–1922), 102.

11. Neil Baxley, *No Prouder Fate: The Story of the 11th South Carolina Volunteer Infantry* (Bloomington, IN: AuthorHouse, 2005), 42.

12. *Official Records of the Union and Confederate Armies, Series 1, Volume 6* (Washington, D.C.: Government Printing Office, 1894–1922), 102.

13. Barbara Tomblin, *Bluejackets and Contrabands: African Americans and the Union Navy* (Lexington, KY: The University Press of Kentucky, 2009), 64.

14. H. David Stone, *Vital Rails: The Charleston & Savannah Railroad and the Civil War in Coastal South Carolina* (Columbia S.C.: University of South Carolina Press, 2008), 93.

15. H. David Stone, *Vital Rails: The Charleston & Savannah Railroad and the Civil War in Coastal South Carolina* (Columbia S.C.: University of South Carolina Press, 2008), 97.

16. "The Civil War," Part 2, in collaboration with Henry Steele Commager, Ph.D. Encyclopedia Britannica Films, Inc.

17. americancivilwar.com/statepic/south_carolina.
html

18. John G. Abbott's Diary, June-September, 1862.

19. Abraham J. Palmer, D.D., *The History of the Forty-Eighth Regiment, New York State Volunteers in the War of the Union, 1861–1865* (Brooklyn, N.Y.: Veterans Association of the Regiment, 1885), 42.

20. John G. Abbott's Diary, May-September, 1862.

21. Abraham J. Palmer, D.D., *The History of the Forty-Eighth Regiment, New York State Volunteers in the War of the Union 1861–1865* (Brooklyn, N.Y.: Veterans Association of the Regiment, 1885), 43.

22. John G. Abbott's Diary, June 18, 1862.

23. Neil Baxley, *No Prouder Fate: The Story of the 11th South Carolina Volunteer Infantry* (Bloomington, IN: AuthorHouse, 2005), 43.

24. Margaret Greer, *The Sands of Time. A History Of Hilton Head Island* (Hilton Head, S.C.: SouthArt, Inc.), 1989, 49.

25. *Official Records of the Union and Confederate Armies, Series 1, Volume 14* (Washington, D.C.: Government Printing Office, 1894–1922), 119.

26. *Official Records of the Union and Confederate Armies, Series 1, Volume 14* (Washington, D.C.: Government Printing Office, 1894–1922), 117.

27. Abraham J. Palmer, D.D., *The History of the Forty-Eighth Regiment, New York State Volunteers in*

the War of the Union 1861–1865 (Brooklyn, N.Y.: Veterans Association of the Regiment, 1885), 46.

28. *Official Records of the Union and Confederate Armies, Series 1, Volume 14* (Washington, D.C.: Government Printing Office, 1894–1922), 125.

29. Congressional Report No. 2584, House of Representatives, 51st Congress, 1st Session (Washington, D.C.: June 27, 1890), 3.

30. John G. Abbott's Diary, September 30, 1862.

31. *Official Records of the Union and Confederate Armies, Series 1, Volume 14* (Washington, D.C.: Government Printing Office, 1894–1922), 126.

32. John G. Abbott's Diary, September 30, 1862.

33. Robert S. Jones, Jr., "Saltworks in the Lowcountry" (*Coastal Angler Magazine*, December 2010).

34. *Official Records of the Union and Confederate Armies, Series 1, Volume 14* (Washington, D.C.: Government Printing Office, 1894–1922), 126.

35. "The Civil War," Part 2, in collaboration with Henry Steele Commager, Ph.D. Encyclopedia Britannica Films, Inc.

36. John G. Abbott's Diary, October 12, 1862.

37. John G. Abbott's Diary, October 18, 1862.

38. John G. Abbott's Diary, October 18, 1862.

39. John G. Abbott's Diary, October 18, 1862.

40. Abraham J. Palmer, D.D., *The History of the Forty Eighth Regiment, New York State Volunteers in the War of the Union 1861–1865* (Brooklyn, N.Y.: Veterans Association of the Regiment, 1885), 46.

41. Frank Moore, *The Rebellion Record: A Diary of American Events, Volume 6* (New York: G.P. Putnam, 1863), 34.

42. John G. Abbott's Diary, October 22, 1862.

43. Frank Moore, *The Rebellion Record: A Diary of American Events, Volume 6* (New York: G.P. Putnam, 1863), 35.

44. H. David Stone, *Vital Rails: The Charleston & Savannah Railroad and the Civil War in Coastal South Carolina* (Columbia, S.C.: University of South Carolina Press, 2008), 64.

45. Emancipation Proclamation, January 1, 1863.

46. Neil Baxley, *No Prouder Fate: The Story of the 11th South Carolina Volunteer Infantry* (Bloomington, IN: AuthorHouse, 2005), 75.

47. John G. Abbott's Diary, March 12, 1863.

48. Neil Baxley, *No Prouder Fate: The Story of the 11th South Carolina Volunteer Infantry* (Bloomington, IN: AuthorHouse, 2005), 79.

VI

The Bluffton Expedition

A portion of a map by George Woolworth, circa 1861. Library of Congress.

The grand and imposing battleship, USS *Wabash,* which led the devastating Union attack against Forts Walker and Beauregard in November of 1861, was moored in Port Royal Harbor. The *Wabash*'s captain, Rear Admiral Samuel Francis DuPont, was residing in his quarters aboard the flagship on or around May 27, 1863, when he received a prioritized naval support request.[1] Major-General David Hunter, whose headquarters were located on Hilton Head, had been planning a key expedition into the strategically located town of Bluffton. What made this mission unique, however, was its objective. Hunter's instructions were lucid and concise; destroy the town of Bluffton by fire.

The combined movement called for 1,000 troops and four coastal vessels. Critical to the accomplishment of the mission, Hunter believed, would be the fire support of a durable naval gunboat capable of riverine operations. At the time DuPont received Hunter's request around May 27 for the assistance of a craft of this type, there were currently none in readiness at Port Royal. This changed on June 3, however, with the availability of the USS *Commodore McDonough,* a coastal gunboat specifically outfitted for this type of incursion.

With a shallow draft of just 8½ feet and a crew of 75 sailors, the *Commodore McDonough,* at 154 feet, could navigate inland waters where naval warships could not venture. She was commissioned in New York in November of 1862, placed under the authority of Lieutenant-Commander George Bacon, and made her eventual arrival at Port Royal in December.[2] Her armament had been altered to some degree since commissioning and now consisted of five heavy guns, including a massive 100 pounder Parrot with a range of over four miles.

HEADQUARTERS OF GENERALS HUNTER AND MITCHEL.

From The History of the Forty-Eighth Regiment.

Aside from Bluffton's national reputation as a hotbed of secessionist activity prior to the outbreak of hostilities, the town now held a military significance as well. Since the fall of Hilton Head, Bluffton had served as a key central outpost from where pickets were distributed to strategic vantage points outlining the greater Bluffton peninsula. This elaborate network of lookouts and couriers provided an early warning system to commanders in Hardeeville. Significant reports often originated from Rebel pickets stationed at Foot Point, or present-day Colleton River Plantation, where the Federal fleet moored in Port Royal Sound was monitored around the clock.[3]

The riverfront Church of the Cross and the neighboring dock at the end of Calhoun Street were often used in conjunction as a picket port. Sergeant Abbott made this observation during a September 1862 reconnaissance of the town.[4] Rowboats and canoes were moored to the dock and utilized by Captain Mickler's company and other units. From this principal outpost, the Rebels launched essential foraging expeditions, scouting missions, and stealthy nighttime raids.

Bluffton's physical outline as an expansive peninsula made it noteworthy from a purely geographical standpoint. If Beauregard's military department could retain control of Bluffton, they would likely maintain a clutch on Buckingham Ferry, the vital central landing point fusing Hilton Head with the mainland. Running generally west from Buckingham through greater Bluffton and roughly parallel with the length of the peninsula was Fording Island Road. Fording Island merged Bluffton with the King's Highway, via other connecter routes.

The King's Highway, a principal stagecoach road, ran somewhat contiguous to the eastern seaboard and linked major cities such as Savannah and Charleston. In addition to Fording Island Road, another key route was May River Road, which originated in Bluffton and ran its course west to Camp Pritchard, eventually making its way down to the low-lying banks of the New River. A narrow wooden bridge was situated at this crossing, forming a funnel and choke point of regional military consequence. Under the direction of General Robert E. Lee, with guidance from resident officers such as General Drayton, the Rebels had constructed earthworks at this site as part of Lee's comprehensive coastal defense network. May River Road, in conjunction with other thoroughfares, was the shortest method of travelling by land from Bluffton to Savannah, via a ferry point set across from Savannah's downtown district.

USS Wabash, Port Royal Harbor, 1863. Courtesy of the United States Naval Historical Society.

With the mission-essential naval gunboat *Commodore McDonough* now at his disposal, Admiral DuPont issued written orders on June 3, 1863, to her captain, Lieutenant-Commander Bacon. In part the orders read: "Sir, Major-General Hunter having requested me to furnish a gunboat to cover the movement of a portion of his land forces, you will report to him that I have assigned you to that duty. You will then proceed with the *Commodore McDonough*, under your command, to Fort Pulaski..."[5]

One of two known flank markers used by the 48th New York Infantry. Courtesy of the New York State Military Museum.

Bacon and his well-trained crew departed Port Royal and reached Fort Pulaski at 4:00 p.m., reporting as ordered to Colonel Barton, who would be commanding the land forces in the expedition against Bluffton. Participating in the operation would be approximately 1,000 fresh soldiers, excluding the 75 sailors manning the *McDonough's* stations or crews aboard the other three vessels. The aggregate Union force was comprised of six companies from the 48th New York, 50 troops each from the 3rd Rhode Island Artillery and the New York Volunteer Engineers, and three Companies from the 115th New York.[6]

That evening on Cockspur Island, Lieutenant-Commander Bacon was updated on the battle plan, and then the companies' leadership, including officers and senior enlisted personnel from both branches, discussed the details of the assignment, issued the troops' ammunition and one day's rations, and made finishing preparations for departure.

According to Hunter's design, four river crafts would partake in the incursion. These boats included the transports *Island City* and *Cossack*, the army gunboat *Mayflower* doubling as a transport, and the brutish-looking naval gunboat *McDonough*. It was pre-arranged that the *McDonough*, a vessel with a slightly deeper draft than the others, would unfasten her lines and cast off early that evening in order to take advantage of the high tides. The *Island City*, *Cossack*, and *Mayflower* would follow momentarily.[7] In line with the plan, the four Federal steamers would then rendezvous at an approximate midway point adjacent to the south end of Hilton Head at 11:30 p.m. The task force would then head towards the point of attack well in advance of first light.

On this damp summer morning, the combined Confederate force stationed on the greater Bluffton mainland was made up of one infantry and four cavalry companies. The cavalry components, headed by Lieutenant-Colonel Thomas H. Johnson, were quartered at Camp Pritchard located near present-day Pritchardville, with an active central outpost established in the town of Bluffton. Johnson's elements consisted of companies A, B, and G, 3rd South Carolina Cavalry, and Company B, 4th South Carolina Cavalry. Company E of the 11th South Carolina

Infantry, commanded by Captain Mickler, was camped in the town along the sheer banks of the river and 300 yards from the wharf.

The early morning hours of June 4, 1863, were notably foggy according to later testimonies of Confederate lookouts who were stationed beside the May River.[8] Peering out through this dense fog from their picket post near present-day Alljoy Landing at Hunting Island Plantation, were two troopers of the 3rd South Carolina Cavalry. One of the soldiers remains unidentified in the official records; the other was listed as Private Savage of Company B. Lieutenant-Colonel Johnson, commanding the 3rd South Carolina Cavalry's Camp Pritchard detachment, later described the whereabouts of Hunting Island Plantation in a report addressed to Captain James Lowndes. Amid some confusion, Johnson specified for the record that Hunting Island Plantation was not an actual island, but was part of the Bluffton mainland: "Hunting Island, which is a part of the main [mainland], from 1½ to 2 miles below [downstream] Bluffton by land and several miles by water in the direction of Buckingham Ferry..."[9]

Meanwhile, as the sun's faint light gradually emerged in the east prior to daybreak, Private Savage and his colleague at their post near Alljoy Landing noticed several large figures materializing from within the dense cloud of moisture hovering over the river. As the dark silhouettes steadily proceeded west, it was soon apparent to the lookouts that they were witnessing Union ships moving upstream towards Bluffton.

As the vessels slowly approached, the troopers counted only three crafts. In fact, their observation was accurate. On the previous evening, as the army gunboat *Mayflower* approached the rendezvous point near the south end of Hilton Head Island in Calibogue Sound, she ran aground and was lodged on either an oyster bank or sand bar. Because the North's scheme called for the ships to set out from the assembly area well before dawn, and because it was determined that the tides would not permit the *Mayflower* to dislodge until approximately sunrise, Lieutenant-Commander Bacon advised Colonel Barton that he could provide adequate fire support with his weapons alone. Bacon concluded that it would be in the mission's best interest to carry on without the *Mayflower*. The captain of the army gunboat was then directed to proceed to the objective at Bluffton and join the action in progress once the tides raised and released his stranded vessel.

As the Rebel duo continued to survey the three boats cruising upstream through the thick mist, they knew that the command's standard operating procedure called for them to immediately notify the 3rd South Carolina Cavalry's Commander of Outposts, as well as the Commander of Company E, 11th South Carolina, camped within the town. Private Savage immediately sent his comrade to warn the commanders in Bluffton.

Shortly after the trooper left to sound the alarm, Savage moved back 150 yards to a wooded stretch in an effort to provide himself with adequate cover and concealment.

From this veiled vantage point, the picket continued to monitor the three steamers when he noticed the two transports angle towards the shoreline. It was now apparent to Savage that the *Island City* and *Cossack* were moving into a landing position alongside the banks of Hunting Island Plantation to allow for the offload of troops. The naval gunboat then assumed a tactical station to safeguard Barton's amphibious landing.

At around 6:00 a.m., as Savage was witnessing the transfer from his masked hide-out, his companion returned with a distressing update; he was unable to locate any coalition units, neither the 3rd South Carolina Cavalry nor the 11th South Carolina Infantry. Time was now of the essence. Savage realized that the critical interval which had lapsed would more than likely result in adverse consequences for the Rebels camped in Bluffton.

USS Commodore McDonough. Courtesy of the United States Naval Historical Society.

*In addition to four other large weapons, the USS Commodore
McDonough was equipped with a powerful 100 pounder Parrot
such as the one seen here at Fort Totten manned by the 3rd
Massachusetts Heavy Artillery. Library of Congress.*

The time was now roughly 6:15 a.m. Private
Savage instructed the other trooper to remain on
post. Savage then effortlessly mounted his horse
and galloped away to notify Lieutenant-Colonel
Johnson at Camp Pritchard.[10] As this act was
unfolding at Hunting Island Plantation,
Confederate lookouts fixed on an observation point
upstream at Baynard's Plantation on May River
Neck, were entirely unaware of their approaching
adversaries. May River Neck, or present-day
Palmetto Bluff, is a peninsula consisting of
approximately 20,000 pristine acres bounded by
the picturesque May, New, and Cooper Rivers.

Of notable worth, Lieutenant-Colonel
Johnson and the majority of his troopers had

only recently arrived at Camp Pritchard and assumed command just days prior. It is uncertain whether Private Savage's comrade's inability to find the Confederates camped in Bluffton this morning was a result of personal irresponsibility, or the lack of sufficient training and familiarization with the area. In contrast, Captain Mickler, a native of Beaufort who had been stationed in Bluffton for some time, was exceedingly familiar with the local geography. Ironically, however, on the preceding evening of June 3, Mickler had left Bluffton and travelled to Hardeeville to inquire with his regimental commander, Colonel Frederick H. Gant, concerning housing for his family. Prior to leaving he designated his executive officer and number two in command, Lieutenant Wilson Smith, as the acting commander of Company E.[11]

Having disembarked a large portion of their 1,000-man force at Hunting Island Plantation, the small squadron under Bacon's command began making its way upstream towards the town. At some point before the gunboat *McDonough* and the two transports *Cossack* and *Island City* reached Buck Point, or present-day Myrtle Island, they were rejoined by the army gunboat *Mayflower*.

As the four ships rounded Myrtle Island at 7:00 a.m., they passed the next Confederate pickets positioned across the estuary at Baynard's on Palmetto Bluff. Conducting surveillance from the lofty bluff at Baynard's, Sergeant Jones, a lookout assigned to Company B, spotted the four vessels at this time. According to Jones, "it was a foggy morning," and after spotting the ships, he "at once dispatched a courier to Lieutenant-Colonel Johnson located at Camp Pritchard."[12]

Camp Pritchard had been established to accommodate a considerable number of troops and would have been sizeable enough to quarter at least 400 men with quite a few horse stables. The camp's perimeter most likely encompassed a large expanse, with individual companies occupying separate cantonment areas. Lieutenant-Colonel Johnson wrote to Captain James Lowndes on June 5, 1863, explaining that Camp Pritchard was positioned roughly equidistant from Bluffton and Hardeeville.[13] In later writings, Richard Coffman, who conducted extensive research on the Phillips Georgia Legion Infantry Battalion, indicated that the camp was located, "...about two miles from the New River Bridge."[14] Both Johnson's and Coffman's descriptions and distances place the site within a ½-mile radius of present-day New Riverside Roundabout.

From his lookout point at Palmetto Bluff, Sergeant Jones was afforded a wide and panoramic view of the river as it hooked around Myrtle Island, then gradually bowed left along the vertical bluffs of Hunting Island Plantation, or Kirk's Bluff, and finally passing the town of Bluffton. Jones cautiously watched as the ships rounded the bend at Myrtle Island and then, "anchored from half to three-quarters of a mile from the town..."[15] From this position, the guns of the *McDonough* and *Mayflower* could provide indirect support to Barton's companies as they rapidly marched towards Bluffton, while also situated with a commanding view of the town and well within artillery range.

A portion of a circa 1861 map by Evans and Cogswell showing May River Neck, or present-day Palmetto Bluff. Library of Congress.

At or around 7:00 a.m., the approximate time in which Sergeant Jones' courier was leaving Palmetto Bluff for Camp Pritchard on horseback, Private Savage, having bypassed Bluffton, arrived at the cavalry encampment and alerted Johnson of the Union Landing. After Savage recounted with bated breath that four ships and a regiment-size force were converging on Bluffton, the bugle was promptly sounded. We can only speculate as to why Private Savage bypassed the cavalry outpost within Bluffton. All pickets had been clearly instructed to report any sightings to the on-duty commander there. Savage may have considered the possibility that his comrade was correct and that there were no Confederates in the town. If indeed his fellow trooper was right, he would have squandered even more valuable time. Nevertheless, Savage took the main route west along May River Road and proceeded directly to Camp Pritchard. There he was assured to find several companies of Rebels to warn.

As the bugler sounded the call to arms with his winded instrument made of brass, Johnson began forming up the cavalry forces present at the site, which consisted of four companies totaling 182 enlisted men and six officers.[16] In the customary procedure, officers and senior enlisted soldiers hastily inspected weapons and equipment.

At around 7:15 a.m., Lieutenant Smith, acting commander of Company E, was beginning to eat breakfast at his campsite in Bluffton on the bank of the river. Because Private Savage had disregarded Bluffton and continued directly to Camp Pritchard to alert Johnson, Smith and his men were oblivious to the fact that two separate contingents of their antagonists were converging upon their position, one by land, the other along the watercourse. Then, startlingly and without warning, one of Smith's infantrymen swiftly approached to sound the alarm; gunboats had been spotted on the May River within shelling distance, and Union soldiers were filing into the town from Hunting Island Plantation.

138 The Bluffton Expedition

Having landed with no opposition at Hunting Island Plantation, the Yankees, primarily of the 48th New York, had formed up and begun a fast-paced and determined march towards the town in several columns. As the companies aggressively swarmed on the abandoned village, they first set fire to several homes on the east side of Heyward Cove along Pritchard Street and near the bank of the river. The initial wafting smoke clouds observed by the Confederates originated from this area adjacent to the homes of Colonel Joseph J. Stoney and Dr. Paul Pritchard.[17] The time was now approximately 7:30 a.m.

Meanwhile Smith had formed up the 50 or so men of Company E, hid any remnants of their personal gear, and hastily marched to May River Road. Smith feared that Federal commanders would attempt to flank his company's position in an effort to cut off their westerly retreat and trap the Rebels along the steep bluffs of the May River.

After posting several scouts in a concealed position in a nearby wooded area to monitor the enemy's movements, Smith quickly marched his men west along May River Road until they were roughly one mile from the town. Here at Sandy Bridge, located at present-day Crooked Cove, Lieutenant Smith deployed his infantrymen in fighting positions on both sides of the road to receive the anticipated Union advance.[18] On previous expeditions Federal forces had frequently marched through the town and slightly beyond. Smith was therefore preparing for a considerable skirmish at Sandy Bridge, unaware that Colonel Barton's 48th New York had no intentions of streaming west past the town. The Yankees were adhering to Hunter's stringent orders to hurriedly ignite Bluffton by torch, and then rendezvous with and quickly board the transports waiting at the wharf.

As Smith and his company of infantry had filed west out of the town, Union troops simultaneously filtered into Bluffton unopposed from the east, branching out in squads along various streets in order to set fire to certain homes. Sergeant Abbott noted, "They [Federals] then fired the town and soon every building was on fire."[19]

As Johnson and his cavalrymen rapidly approached the town on horseback, they discovered Smith's company crouched in a defensive position at Sandy Bridge. With these two units now joined by around 8:30 a.m., a respectful-sized Confederate force had amassed. Johnson had accumulated a 238-man Rebel defense, and even though the 1,000-man Union contingent led by Colonel Barton outnumbered the Confederates four to one, four companies of cavalry were a formidable threat to any foe.

The four river crafts that had anchored just over ½ mile from the town now began pulling up their weighty mooring devices in order to move closer to Bluffton. Lieutenant-Commander Bacon explained: "I moved up with this vessel [McDonough] and the transports for the purpose of being better able to cover their movements, as well as to be ready to re-embark the troops in case of necessity, as the enemy had mustered quite a large force in the rear of the town of infantry and cavalry."[20]

The two bulky Federal gunboats making their way up the May River were quite a daunting threat to the Confederates, and an invaluable asset to Union troops on the ground. The *McDonough's* armament alone consisted of the following artillery: one 100 pounder Parrot with a range of over four miles; one nine-inch Dahlgren smoothbore shell gun with a maximum range of two miles; two smoothbore howitzers with an effective range of just over 1,000 yards; and a 50 pounder rifled Dahlgren with a range of over 3,000 yards.

Before a single shot was fired in the expedition against Bluffton, the Union commanded certain tactical advantages from the outset. The town's narrow roads bordered by homes or wood lines produced tight quarters for battle and diminished the potential effectiveness of the Confederate cavalry, which would theoretically enhance the already superior Yankee numbers. Secondly, the *McDonough* and the *Mayflower* were capable of providing overwhelming direct and indirect fire support to Federal troops on the ground, producing what is known as a force multiplier.

At Sandy Bridge west of Bluffton, Smith began to brief Johnson on the situation in the town. He explained that gunboats were at the bluff and that the enemy was already roving through the neighborhoods. Johnson later wrote that he then "ordered this company, under Lieutenant Smith, forward [east towards Bluffton] as skirmishers, and sent two cavalrymen, dismounted, in advance as scouts."[21] Johnson also reported that he instructed Smith to engage the enemy and hold his position until support from the cavalry arrived. Smith disputed this claim, stating that he was ordered to advance, make contact with the superior-sized enemy force, and then fall back until supported.

According to Union accounts, the Confederates exchanged small arms fire with Union soldiers three times between 8:30 a.m. and 12:00 p.m. The first contact was initiated by Smith and his infantry, with several of Johnson's scouts dismounted in support. This minor skirmish took place in the "bend" along May River Road on the outskirts of town. As the Confederates were approaching this location, they soon spotted "...25 or 30 [Federals] in number, whom they fired on, which fire was promptly returned by the enemy, and at this point the gunboats commenced shelling."[22]

In addition to the challenge of facing an overwhelming opponent supported by two patrol boats, the Rebels now encountered another obstacle; most of Bluffton was engulfed in flames by mid-morning. Amid the sizzling blaze, the Rebels charged south along the street leading to the wharf, where they came into contact with Barton's rear guard, which was maintaining a defensive posture while the remainder of the 48th New York began climbing aboard the transports.

Each time the gray-clad soldiers made contact with the boys in blue, the Rebels encountered not only musket volleys, but also artillery salvoes from the *McDonough* and the *Mayflower*. According to Lieutenant-Commander Bacon aboard the *Commodore McDonough*, on the Confederate's final surge, "The enemy advanced down the street leading to the wharf through the town, expecting no doubt to sweep off in the general rush the few [rear guard] who were covering the reembarkation, as they were in considerable force by that time. They charged with cheers [rebel yells] to within a short distance of the steamers, when, from their repeated volleys, we got their position (as at that time we were unable to distinguish any object, not even the steamers or our own troops, owing to the dense volumes of smoke which were settling over the river), when we opened with shrapnel and shell in the direction of the enemy, and the effect was instantaneous, as I have since been assured by the commander of the land forces that our shrapnel and shell passed directly over the heads of our men, exploding in front of the ranks of the enemy, causing them to break and retreat in disorder "[23]

As the morning progressed, the heavy fog lingering over the river had lifted, and was now replaced with dense smoke billowing from the burning homes. The weather was "clear and warm," according to Sergeant Abbott's diary entry.[24] The blistering inferno consuming the village only served to compound the heat of the day, which was now being felt by the fighters dressed in thick wool blend uniforms and carrying only a limited quantity of water.

No record exists of how many shells were fired from the *Mayflower*, but according to Bacon the *McDonough* alone expended 143 rounds. Bacon also recounted that the *Mayflower*'s weapons were active as well. It is probable that the Mayflower depleted at least 60 rounds, bringing the total estimated expenditures at well over 200 artillery shells fired from the two patrol boats.

The intensity of such concentrated firepower in a relatively small area proved to be an enormous impediment to the Confederate charges. Of the four types of artillery aboard the *McDonough*, it was the howitzers that proved most effective against the Rebels on this day. The howitzer had been used throughout the war by artillerists as a medium between long-ranged rifled weapons and light Coehorn mortars with a high arch. Nearly 100 of the 143 rounds spent from the naval gunboat came from two howitzers, and most of these were in the form of deadly shrapnel or canisters.[25] The howitzers effectively kept the Confederates at a standoff distance by raining down a torrent of deadly shrapnel and canister shot. The shells were equipped with fuse delays that triggered the explosion of the spherical ordnance at a predetermined time. The canisters consisted of a cylindrical-shaped shell packed with numerous golf-ball-sized shot. When fired, this deadly and intimidating weapon mimicked a giant shotgun blast that sent a lethal shower downrange, blanketing an area. These munitions and the tactics used by the Union proved effective in halting the initial Rebel advance east along May River Road, as well as the final charge south down the street leading to the wharf.

Having heard of the Union landing from one of Johnson's couriers who was sent to warn Hardeeville, Captain Mickler rode for 16 miles at the maximum rate of speed his horse could safely endure. After arriving at Sandy Bridge at roughly 11:30 a.m. and finding Johnson's men halted,

Mickler immediately moved forward to Bluffton, took control of his company, and then advanced through the fire and smoke to the wharf.

When Mickler and his infantry reached the bluff just before 12:00 p.m., Colonel Barton had already boarded his troops and the ships were gently rounding the bend in the May River. As the vessels drifted around the arc, Mickler made a desperate attempt to strike his antagonist who had fired the town, quickly leading several sharpshooters along a shortcut in an effort to waylay the boats as they passed. The Rebels arrived too late, however, as the small squadron had already passed the planned ambush site.[26]

According to Confederate lookout Sergeant Jones of Company B, stationed at Baynard's Plantation on Palmetto Bluff, the boats crept between his position and Myrtle Island at approximately 12:30 p.m. Private Savage, the picket who had been stationed near Alljoy Landing that morning, reported that he returned to his Hunting Island Plantation post at 2:00 p.m., and that the ships had already departed prior to that time.

Upon retiring from Bluffton, the six companies of the 48th New York returned to Fort Pulaski aboard the *Cossack*. The *Island City* and *Mayflower* steamed to Hilton Head to offload companies of the 115th New York, before continuing to Pulaski with members of the 3rd Rhode Island Artillery and the New York Volunteer Engineers.[27] That afternoon, from his stateroom aboard the *McDonough* now moored in Port Royal, Lieutenant-Commander George Bacon penned a brief summary to Rear-Admiral DuPont: "In conclusion, I beg leave to state that the expedition was a complete success, which I consider owing to the hearty cooperation of both branches of the service."28 He goes on to credit Colonel Barton and the 48th New York, as well as his ship's crew, for their professionalism and skill that was demonstrated throughout the engagement.

Initial casualty reports were astoundingly low; in a June 5 memo, Lieutenant-Colonel Thomas H. Johnson lists one Confederate soldier wounded from an artillery shell fired from the gunboats.29 Several days later while at Fort Pulaski, members of the 48th New York were informed that the Confederates suffered two killed and one wounded in the skirmish.30

Military inquiries into the conduct of officers and enlisted personnel following engagements were not uncommon during the war. The burning of Bluffton was a high-profile incident with numerous high-ranking officers losing their homes in the blaze, and the discrepancy between Johnson's and Smith's accounts gave additional cause for their superiors to explore their actions in more depth.

The investigation conducted by Captain John F. Lay, Assistant Adjutant General, reveals that Johnson was slow to advance and provide support to Smith. Lay felt that both Confederate commanders, however, could have progressed and engaged the Yankees sooner. Lay's harshest criticism was directed at the trooper who accompanied Private Savage at the picket post near Alljoy Landing. This soldier failed to notify the commander of outposts in Bluffton and the duty officer at Camp Pritchard of the approaching Union force. Immediately after the initial investigation, Captain Lay ordered this unnamed soldier arrested for failure to carry out his official duties. Lay then made a recommendation to General Jordan "that charges be preferred against him."[31]

The judgments made by Johnson and Smith and their subsequent actions on June 4 would have been based on additional factors that are imperative to point out. Their primary mission was not the defense of Bluffton. As detachment commander at Camp Pritchard, Johnson commanded all cavalry forces between Bluffton and the New River Bridge. Reliable and accurate intelligence reports from several lookouts had numbered the enemy's strength at around 1,000 troops, with a force multiplier of two gunboats within shelling range. In theory, an overly aggressive maneuver by the Confederates, coupled with an effective flank by Barton's 48th New York, could have resulted in the capture or loss of the entire Rebel force.

The primary mission of the Confederates stationed in the lowcountry was to defend the cities of Charleston and Savannah and the vital railroad that linked these urban strongholds. The strategy incorporated to accomplish this regional mission was initially devised and implemented by General Robert E. Lee, and later continued by Generals Pemberton and Beauregard. This plan called for slowing the inland advance of amphibious forces through a network of defenses stationed along routes leading from the coast.

If Major-General David Hunter's objective had been to drive Colonel Barton's 48th through Bluffton in an effort to march to Hardeeville and destroy the railroad there, he would have encountered several obstacles along the route. The first such impediment would have been the Sandy Bridge crossing at Crooked Cove, where Company E first halted and took up fighting positions on the morning of June 4.

Confederate commanders including Johnson and Smith understood the value of the Charleston and Savannah Railroad and the policy General Lee developed to shield it. If the 48th New York had succeeded in advancing along May River Road as far as the New River Bridge, Barton would have had to contend with earthworks and a formidable battery there. The establishment of fortifications at this site indicates the position would have been defended at high costs, resulting in a significant battle.

Whether or not Captain Mickler's presence on the morning of June 4 would have contributed to a variance in the day's outcome is uncertain. Mickler was a capable, aggressive, and wily tactician, and his brave team of enlisted scouts was no less impressive. Their effectiveness while conducting scouting patrols and their success using guerilla-style tactics throughout the islands surrounding Bluffton had garnered high praise.

Neil Baxley, author of *No Prouder Fate: The Story of the 11th South Carolina Volunteer Infantry*, has conducted extensive research on the 11th South Carolina, to include Company E. Baxley believes that based on Captain Mickler's previous record, had he been present in Bluffton on the morning of June 4, 1863, the resultant skirmish would have likely been altered. Baxley valuates that Mickler's presence could have resulted in a higher casualty count for both aggressor and defender.[32]

Captain Lay revealed the findings of his initial investigation into the burning of Bluffton in a letter written on June 20 to Brigadier-General Thomas Jordon, Chief of Staff. From his headquarters in Charleston on June 30, 1863, General P.G.T. Beauregard reviewed Lay's assessment and the reports of those involved in the June 4 skirmish. Beauregard forwarded Lay's discoveries to Secretary J.A. Seddon and noted that: "A court of inquiry has been asked for by Lieutenant-Colonel Johnson, and will be given him, to inquire into his conduct on this occasion."[33] According to official records, Johnson submitted a subsequent application requesting a court of inquiry into his own actions. "On August 17, 1863, Lieutenant-Colonel Johnson renewed application for a court of inquiry, and in reply on August 20th, was informed that no court would be convened until it could be done without detriment to the service."[34]

The expedition against Bluffton had drawn to a conclusion. As Barton and his 48th New York were making the intercoastal passage back to Fort Pulaski on the afternoon of June 4, Johnson, Mickler, and their bushed troops were struggling to extinguish the flames still soaring from the burning buildings. The profuse smoke clouds drifting from the town were witnessed from miles away.

Not far from the searing firestorm, the Secession Oak, under whose canopy the Bluffton Movement originated, had survived the blaze. By the afternoon, reports of the burning of Bluffton were being transmitted along telegraph wires throughout the South. The name had first represented a town, then a nationally recognized movement calling for secession. Rhett's "Bluffton" was in ashes.

The Secession Oak. Photograph by Jeff Fulgham.

Chapter VI Source Notes

1. *Official Records of the Union and Confederate Navies, Series 1, Volume 14* (Washington, D.C.: Government Printing Office, 1894–1922), 237.

2. Dictionary of American Naval Fighting Ships (DANFS) http://www.history.navy.mil/danfs/c12/commodore_mcdonough.htm

3. Lloyd Halliburton, *Saddle Soldiers: The Civil War Correspondence of General William Stokes of the 4th South Carolina Cavalry* (Orangeburg, S.C.: Sandlapper Publishing Company, Inc., 1993), 71, 72.

4. John G. Abbott's Diary, September 30, 1862.

5. *Official Records of the Union and Confederate Navies, Series 1, Volume 14* (Washington, D.C.: Government Printing Office, 1894–1922), 236.

6. John G. Abbott's Diary, June 3, 1863.

7. John G. Abbott's Diary, June 3, 1863.

8. *Official Records of the Union and Confederate Armies, Series 1, Volume 14* (Washington, D.C.: Government Printing Office, 1894–1922), 311.

9. *Official Records of the Union and Confederate Armies, Series 1, Volume 14* (Washington, D.C.: Government Printing Office, 1894–1922), 309.

10. *Official Records of the Union and Confederate Armies, Series 1, Volume 14* (Washington, D.C.: Government Printing Office, 1894–1922), 309, 311.

11. *Official Records of the Union and Confederate Armies, Series 1, Volume 14* (Washington, D.C.: Government Printing Office, 1894–1922), 311.

12. *Official Records of the Union and Confederate Armies, Series 1, Volume 14* (Washington, D.C.: Government Printing Office, 1894–1922), 310.

13. *Official Records of the Union and Confederate Armies Series 1, Volume 14* (Washington, D.C.: Government Printing Office, 1894–1922), 309, 310.

14. Richard M. Coffman and Kurt D. Graham, *To Honor These Men: a History of the Phillips Georgia Legion Infantry Battalion* (Macon, GA.: Mercer University Press, 2007), 68.

15. *Official Records of the Union and Confederate Navies, Series 1, Volume 14* (Washington, D.C.: Government Printing Office, 1894–1922), 238.

16. *Official Records of the Union and Confederate Armies, Series 1, Volume 14* (Washington, D.C.: Government Printing Office, 1894–1922), 309.

17. *Charleston Mercury*, June 6, 1863.

18. *Official Records of the Union and Confederate Armies, Series 1, Volume 14* (Washington, D.C.: Government Printing Office, 1894–1922), 312.

19. John G. Abbott's Diary, June 4, 1863.

20. *Official Records of the Union and Confederate Navies, Series 1, Volume 14* (Washington, D.C.: Government Printing Office, 1894–1922), 238.

21. *Official Records of the Union and Confederate Armies, Series 1, Volume 14* (Washington, D.C.: Government Printing Office, 1894–1922), 309.

22. *Official Records of the Union and Confederate Armies, Series 1, Volume 14* (Washington, D.C.: Government Printing Office, 1894–1922), 309, 312.

23. *Official Records of the Union and Confederate Navies, Series 1, Volume 14* (Washington, D.C.: Government Printing Office, 1894–1922), 239.

24. John G. Abbott's Diary, June 4, 1863.

25. *Official Records of the Union and Confederate Navies, Series 1, Volume 14* (Washington, D.C.: Government Printing Office, 1894–1922), 239.

26. *Official Records of the Union and Confederate Armies, Series 1, Volume 14* (Washington, D.C.: Government Printing Office, 1894–1922), 314.

27. John G. Abbott's Diary, June 4, 1863.

28. *Official Records of the Union and Confederate Navies, Series 1, Volume 14* (Washington, D.C.: Government Printing Office, 1894–1922), 239.

29. *Official Records of the Union and Confederate Armies, Series 1, Volume 14* (Washington, D.C.: Government Printing Office, 1894–1922), 310.

30. John G. Abbott's Diary, June 10, 1863.

31. *Official Records of the Union and Confederate Armies, Series 1, Volume 14* (Washington, D.C.: Government Printing Office, 1894–1922), 314.

32. Neil Baxley's Letter to Jeff Fulgham, August 9, 2011.

33. *Official Records of the Union and Confederate Armies, Series 1, Volume 14* (Washington, D.C.: Government Printing Office, 1894–1922), 310.

34. *Official Records of the Union and Confederate Armies, Series 1, Volume 14* (Washington, D.C.: Government Printing Office, 1894–1922), 310.

VII

The Ashes of Bluffton and the Dawn of a New Era

When the sun rose on the morning of June 5, 1863, it was evident that Bluffton's affluent antebellum way of life had vanished forever. Perhaps in an omen of what was to come for the South, the burning of Bluffton was a prelude to the farewell of the Southern plantation era and of the institution of slavery.

Prior to the expedition against Bluffton there were approximately 60 dwellings standing in the town; when the smoldering ruins had cooled, only a fraction of that number remained. On June 6, a *Charleston Mercury* article reported that approximately 40 private residences as well as numerous small buildings and sheds had been destroyed.[1] A dispatch written by Lieutenant-Colonel Johnson suggests that particular homes were targeted. "I suppose one-half or two-thirds of the town has been destroyed, including some of the best buildings, which appear to have been selected."[2]

The headline of an article printed in the *Richmond Dispatch* describing the incident read, "From South Carolina—the town of Bluffton fired by the Yankees." The journalist expounded: "An official dispatch from W.S. Walker, at Pocotaligo, reports that the enemy fired the town of Bluffton today. Our forces engaged them and prevented a further advance."[3] Captain John F. Lay, in a letter penned to his superiors from his headquarters in Charleston on June 20, 1863, stated: "The ashes of Bluffton, with its withered and scorched remains of noble trees and beautiful shrubbery, present a sad scene of desolation and fiendish vandalism unparalleled in the history of civilized nations."[4]

Union commanders, however, including Major-General Hunter and Rear-Admiral DuPont, asserted that the Confederates had been utilizing Bluffton and several of its homes as a central picket headquarters. The town was consequently, in their estimation, a legitimate military target. Commanders from the North and South generally agreed that property used for military purposes was a valid object of attack. Destroying innocent civilian property, however, was commonly frowned upon and considered an unacceptable practice by most officers of the era.

The town of Bluffton held both a military and geo-political significance. Captain Mickler and his small band of fearless scouts had become a hazardous thorn in the side of Hunter's considerably larger force on Hilton Head. Company E was a veritable threat. From raids and captures, to deadly ambushes, this small infantry company had been effective in using unconventional tactics against a bigger and better equipped rival.

Historian Robert Jones, Jr., who served as the executive director of the Bluffton Historical Preservation Society, offers several insightful views on the subject of why Bluffton was attacked. In addition to the grounds already cited, Jones suggests that the incursion could have also served as a distraction while the Union was preparing for a major offensive at Charleston Harbor. Abraham J. Palmer, who served as a private in the 48th New York and ultimately wrote the regiment's history, noted: "The second expedition burned about two-thirds of the town by command of Major-General Hunter, in retaliation for certain unwarlike depredations by the enemy."[5] Palmer was likely referring to the guerrilla-style tactics and unconventional raids that were being effectively carried out by Captain Mickler and his bold scouts.

Broadening the scope of inquiry, to include Hunter's motives and strategic objectives, offers additional explanations concerning Bluffton's destruction. Prior to the burning of Bluffton, Hunter ordered a raid along the Combahee River, a stream emptying into St. Helena Sound north of Beaufort. The expedition was commanded by Colonel James Montgomery. Assisting Montgomery as a liaison between black scouts and Union officers was abolitionist Harriet Tubman.[6] In this incursion on June 2, 1863, hundreds of slaves were taken away from their respective plantations and a considerable amount of civilian property was scorched by orders of David Hunter.

After the damaging raid on the Combahee and the burning of Bluffton, Hunter then ordered the destruction of Darien, Georgia, by fire. This action was conducted on June 11. The raid was led by Colonel Montgomery and carried out by companies from two units of African-American descent: the 54th Massachusetts Regiment and the 2nd Regiment

South Carolina Infantry.[7] Neither of these units, however, participated in the expedition against Bluffton.

These operations became widely known as "Hunter's Raids." From his headquarters on Hilton Head Island, Hunter composed a letter to the Secretary of War, E. M. Stanton, on June 3, 1863. This revealing correspondence explains the purpose of the incursions:

Honorable E. M. STANTON,
Secretary of War, Washington, D. C.:

Sir: I have much pleasure in transmitting to you herewith certified copy of a telegraphic report just received from Colonel James Montgomery, commanding Second South Carolina Regiment, of the result of the first of a series of raids upon the main-land, now organized and in process of being carried out. From the report you will see that Colonel Montgomery, with 300 men of his regiment and a section of the Third Rhode Island Battery, commanded by Captain Brayton, penetrated the country of the enemy 25 miles, destroyed a pontoon bridge across the Combahee River, together with a vast amount of cotton, rice, and other property, and brought away with him 725 slaves and some 5 horses. This expedition is but the initial experiment of a system of incursions which will penetrate up all the inlets, creeks and rivers of this department, and to be used in which I am now having several of our light draught transport steamers supplied with bulwarks of boiler iron to protect the troops on board from musketry and rifles; such steamers carrying 10 and 20-pounder howitzers in their bows. I have also to report that Colonel Hawley, Seventh

Regiment Connecticut Volunteers, commanding Saint Augustine, recently made a raid into the interior, in which he captured 118 head of cattle and many mules and horses, the cattle belonging to one Feitch, who was a contractor for supplying beef to the rebel army. Colonel Montgomery with his forces will repeat his incursions as rapidly as possible in different directions, injuring the enemy all he can and carrying away their slaves, thus rapidly filling up the South Carolina regiments in the departments, of which there are now four. The Fifty-fourth Massachusetts regiment (colored), Colonel Shaw commanding, arrived today in good condition, and appears to be an excellent regiment, over 900 strong. They will soon have abundant and very important employment, as will all other regiments, white or colored, that may be sent to reinforce this department. Congratulating you and the country on the favorable aspect of affairs in the Southwest, and hoping soon to be in a position to send you good news from this department, I have the honor to be, sir, with the highest esteem, your very obedient servant,

D. HUNTER, Major-General, Commanding[8]

Prior to his practice of using the torch as a preferred weapon of war, several of David Hunter's foregoing decisions had been controversial. His judgment to emancipate the slaves on his terms, without notice, rather than coordinating his announcement with the president's structured plan, had placed into question his obedience and adherence to the standards of military propriety. Major-General Hunter's actions had stunned his comrades and infuriated his adversaries. Confederate President Jefferson Davis even offered a "...bounty for his capture and execution."9

Hunter's conduct had a polarizing effect on his professional relationship with the president and other Union commanders. Lincoln concluded that the general's activities in South Carolina were counterproductive to the war effort. Furthermore, under Hunter's leadership, the Union's Department of the South had been largely ineffective and had made minimal progress against the Confederate forces of the lowcountry. Just one day prior to the burning of Bluffton, and on the same day Hunter composed a message to inform the Secretary of War of his intended raids, President Lincoln abruptly issued orders directing that Hunter be relieved of command. "On June 3rd the orders were issued for General Gillmore to succeed Major-General Hunter, and on June 12th Gillmore reached Hilton Head, and immediately assumed command."10

In response to his dismissal, the following letter dated June 25, 1863, was written by Hunter and addressed to President Lincoln:11

PRINCETON, N. J., June 25, 1863
His Excellency ABRAHAM LINCOLN,

President of the United States:

SIR: You cannot fail to be aware that my removal from the command of the Department of the South has been all but universally regarded as a censure on my conduct while in that command.

Satisfied and well knowing that I acted throughout in strict obedience to orders, and that my record when published will prove an ample vindication of my course, I now respectfully request of you liberty to make such publication of official documents and records as may be necessary to set me right in the eyes of my friends and in the justice of history. The time has now passed when any injurious effect to the public service could possibly arise from such publication.

Knowing how greatly your time is occupied, I shall regard your silence in reply to this note as giving me the liberty I ask and will act accordingly. Should you deem such publications as I propose unadvisable, will you be kind enough to notify me of your opinion without delay.

I have the honor to be, sir, very respectfully, your most obedient servant,

D. Hunter,
Major- General

Lincoln's response:

Executive Mansion
Washington, June 30, 1863

Major-General Hunter:

My Dear General: I have just received your letter of the 25th of June.

I assure you, and you may feel authorized in stating, that the recent change of commanders in the Department of the South was made for no reasons which, convey any imputation upon your known energy, efficiency, and patriotism; but for causes which seemed sufficient, while they were in no degree incompatible with the respect and esteem which I have always held you as a man and an officer.

I cannot, by giving my consent to a publication of whose details I know nothing, assume the responsibility of whatever you may write. In this matter your own sense of military propriety must be your guide and the regulations of the service your rule of conduct.

I am, very truly, your friend,
A. Lincoln

"Hunter's Raid" on the Combahee River, June 2, 1863. Harper's Weekly.

Major-General David Hunter. Library of Congress.

The burning of Bluffton was a noteworthy Federal operation. Unlike the majority of Civil War actions, senior officials in Washington were quickly advised of Bluffton's destruction. From his stateroom aboard the flagship *Wabash* in Port Royal Harbor on June 6, 1863, Rear Admiral DuPont prepared a brief for the Honorable Gideon Welles, Secretary of the Navy: "This town [Bluffton] has been the headquarters for the Rebels for a long time in this vicinity, from which pickets were distributed at various points."[12] DuPont also confirmed that Bluffton had been intentionally burned: "By the orders of Colonel Barton the town was destroyed by fire, the church only being spared, and though the troops made several charges they were driven back by the troops and the shells and shrapnel of the Commodore McDonough."[13]

On December 7, six months after the expedition against Bluffton, Gideon Welles submitted his Report of the Secretary of the Navy to President Lincoln. Bound within this annual compilation of noteworthy actions, the secretary included information on the "Expedition against Bluffton, South Carolina," which contained the letters of Rear-Admiral DuPont and Lieutenant-Commander Bacon. President Lincoln then incorporated the secretary's document with his Message of the President of the United States that was delivered to the Thirty-Eighth Congress.[14] Official reports on the burning of Bluffton, therefore, had been funneled through the highest military and civilian channels within the Federal government.

Gideon Welles, Secretary of the Navy.
National Archives and Records Administration.

"Hunter's Raids" along the coast came more than a year in advance of William Tecumseh Sherman's destructive march to the sea through Georgia. Although Sherman's policies resulted in copious devastation of civilian property in the last year of the war, President Lincoln's initial military and political strategy at the outset of the conflict was moderate in comparison. During the opening stages of the struggle, public opinion throughout the North concerning the rules of war was somewhat restrained as well. The rampant destruction of private property by fire was not commonly accepted at the outbreak of hostilities. As the deadly and taxing war raged on, however, many Northerners grew weary and were eager to put an end to a conflict that had come with an inordinate cost in terms of human life on both sides.

Lincoln's initial moderate stance is well documented. Most historians agree that the president's principal and foremost objective was to maintain the fragile Union. In H.G. Wells' classic, *A Short History of the World*, the author wrote: "When in the open stages of the war Congress and the Federal generals embarked upon a precipitate emancipation, Lincoln opposed and mitigated their enthusiasm."[15] This list of "Federal generals" in which Wells refers to in his analysis would have certainly included Major-General David Hunter.

After his removal from authority in South Carolina, Hunter was eventually reassigned as commander of the Army of the Shenandoah in western Virginia. Predictably, his deliberate use of the unrelenting torch as a weapon continued, which included the burnings of homes, buildings, and the Virginia Military Institute.

After the burning of Bluffton, crucial battles stormed on throughout the states in 1863. In early July, around the time of the Union siege of Vicksburg, General Robert E. Lee faced Major-General George G. Meade at Gettysburg, Pennsylvania. In a blood-stained and decisive clash that many consider to be the turning point in the war, the Rebels' "...defeat was one which all but sealed the fate of the Confederacy."[16]

On July 4, 1863, General Beauregard, still outraged over the burnings of Bluffton and Darien, penned a letter to Union Brigadier-General Quincy A. Gillmore from his headquarters in Charleston. "In the interest of humanity, it seems to be my duty to address you, with a view of effecting some understanding as to the future conduct of the war in this quarter."[17] Beauregard denunciated Hunter's actions, of which he believed, were violations of the laws of civilized nations. The Confederate general then conveyed his expectation that Gillmore, who had assumed Hunter's assignment as commander of the Department of the South, would properly recognize and honor these generally excepted statutes. Beauregard then scornfully equated "Hunter's Raids" to the British burnings of American property during the War of 1812. In closing, Beauregard inquires as to whether Gillmore believes that the burnings of Bluffton and Darien were "legitimate measures of war" that could be repeated in future actions.[18]

General P.G.T. Beauregard, C.S.A. Library of Congress.

Days later, Brigadier-General Gillmore responded. Firing back with a sharp retort, the Ohio native challenged Beauregard to adhere to the precise system of regulations that he himself was demanding. "I will simply state that, while I shall scrupulously endeavor to conduct the war upon principles well established by usage among civilized nations, I shall also expect from the commanding general opposed to me a full compliance with the same rules and maxims in their unrestricted application to all the forces under my command."[19]

During this vehement correspondence between the generals, the Union was simultaneously intensifying its attacks on the defenses of Charleston with the more capable Gillmore now in command of the Department of the South. In a series of notable engagements from April through September, the Union continued its assault on the key forts of Moultrie, Sumter, and Wagner. Naval bombardments led by Northern ironclads were repulsed, however, by the effective fire of the Confederate garrison at Fort Sumter and the supporting batteries located on Sullivan's and Morris Islands.

Eventually the Union army landed and fought to establish a critical beachhead on the south end of Morris Island on July 10, 1863. The North's primary objective was to dislodge the resolute Confederates from the ominous Fort Wagner. In two perilous attempts to take the fort by direct assault, Union soldiers desperately charged with fixed bayonets, but were overwhelmed and driven back with heavy losses after intense hand-to-hand fighting.

During the second and most noteworthy assault on Fort Wagner, several waves of regiments led by the 54th Massachusetts rushed the fort on the evening of July 18. After dauntlessly charging with fixed bayonets through a hail of Confederate fire, the 54th finally reached the base of the fort's earthworks. A few soldiers managed to mount the parapet where a hand-to-hand struggle ensued. According to Captain Luis F. Emilio, a company commander with the 54th who took part in the assault, "All these events, however, had occurred in a very brief period of time, and the Fifty-Fourth had been repulsed before the arrival of the main portion of Strong's brigade."[20] The bulk of the rigorous and costly fighting had yet to commence. The next waves, which included the 6th Connecticut and then the 48th New York, charged Wagner across the sandy beach through a torrent of artillery and musket fire. After reaching and then scaling the walls, these regiments successfully gained access to the fort after a forceful melee.

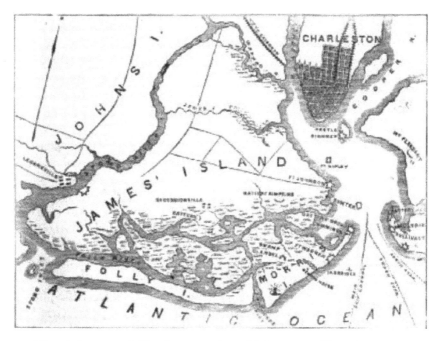

The defenses of Charleston, circa 1864. From The History of the Forty-Eighth Regiment.

The 6th Connecticut and the 48th New York now held a small sector within the fort. Eventually, 140 of these Union soldiers were captured inside Fort Wagner after a lengthy and brutal close-quarters fight lasting several hours. The Confederates had fought with an unwavering determination to defend the fort, "...with the tenacity of bulldogs and a fierce courage..."[21] The Southerners eventually repelled the Yankees.

According to the *Official Records*, the 48th New York suffered more killed in action during the assault than any other regiment involved. Of the 246 Union troops reported killed, 54 belonged to the 48th New York.[22] A total of 10 Northern regiments suffered approximately 1,500 casualties in the assault, while the Rebels suffered over 200 killed, wounded, or missing during their staunch defense of Wagner.

Among the many wounded on Morris Island was Sergeant John G. Abbott from the 48th New York. Abbott was soon transported by ship with other wounded soldiers to Fort Schuyler, New York. In a hospital there, he died of his wounds at age 25 in dramatic fashion while dictating his last diary entry: "P.S. Say to the people of Mays Landing [New Jersey] that I died at my post. When I joined the Army I was willing to die for my country, and to prove my devotion to the flag. It demanded my life which I willingly give."[23] Sergeant Abbott had faithfully kept up his diary entries throughout the war, including his chronicle of the burning of Bluffton on June 4, 1863. The Abbott Diary has since become an important and enduring contribution to American history.

On the day following the assault on Fort Wagner, the 140 Union prisoners captured inside the fort were ferried across the harbor to Charleston. "Forced to march through the streets of the city en route to the jail, the captured soldiers were mocked and cursed by an infuriated mob of townspeople."[24] General Beauregard immediately summoned several of the detainees to determine which regiments had attempted to seize Fort Wagner. After discovering that many of the prisoners were attached to the 48th New York, Beauregard threatened punishment in retaliation for their hand in the burning of Bluffton.[25]

On the night of September 6, 1863, the Confederate garrison within Fort Wagner began evacuating Morris Island as a result of increasing pressures from the encroaching Union siege works. The indomitable Fort Wagner was therefore never taken by direct assault. Fort Sumter, the durable fortress that boldly stood watch over Charleston Harbor, remained a Confederate stronghold for some time.

In November of 1863, Abraham Lincoln presented his now well-known Gettysburg Address on the consecrated battlefield where so many soldiers had perished months earlier. In this speech given on November 19, the president honored the sacrifices of those who had fallen to rest on the surrounding soil: "...that we here highly resolve that these dead shall not have died in vain—that this Nation, under God, shall have a new birth of freedom—and that government of the people, by the people, for the people, shall not perish from the earth."[26]

In 1864 the Department of the South continued to probe the rivers and creeks of the South Carolina lowcountry in an ongoing and demanding effort to reach and sever the Charleston and Savannah Railroad. As General Sherman's far-reaching and devastating army was trudging from Atlanta to Savannah, a significant, but little heralded battle occurred just north of Bluffton at a distance equivalent to a 22-mile march. On November 30, 1864, Union General John P. Hatch, with a force of 5,500 men, assaulted the Confederate earthworks known as Honey Hill situated east of Grahamville.

General Hatch's large contingent, which included several New York and Massachusetts regiments, had departed Hilton Head Island in riverboats and journeyed northwest up the Broad River. The Union's objective called for disembarking at Boyd's Landing and eventually marching generally west along Honey Hill Road to Grahamville. There they would attempt to destroy the Rebel's critical lifeline that linked Charleston and Savannah.

The Federal mission was plagued with navigational glitches from the outset, from low visibility along the watercourse, to inexperienced scouts and inadequate maps. As a result of these crucial delays in the Union advance, Confederate reinforcements arrived in time by rail at Grahamville, including a strong contingent of the Georgia Militia. Upon arrival, Major-General Gustavus Woodson Smith of the Georgia State Militia wisely deferred command at Honey Hill to Colonel Charles Jones Colcock. Colcock, who commanded the 3rd South Carolina Cavalry Regiment, was more knowledgeable of the local topography than Woodson. As the leading Union elements finally began pressing forward along the road to Grahamville, they approached the well-designed earthworks at Honey Hill, which the Rebels had now reinforced in preparation for the anticipated assault.

The overall Confederate force numbered less than 2,000, but they held a superior fortified position and effectively repelled several Union charges with deadly effect. The Yankees were forced to retreat, but not before taking considerable losses. "The Union had suffered more than 750 killed, wounded, or missing. By comparison the South counted only 50 casualties among the units who reported."27

Several factors contributed to the South's victory at Honey Hill. Rebel cavalry forces hampered the already much delayed Union advance, while the Charleston and Savannah Railroad enabled Confederate commanders to shift reinforcements to Grahamville. As part of the series of coastal earthworks established or reinforced under the direction of Robert E. Lee, the well-positioned Honey Hill and the gritty combatants within had stymied the Federals' inland thrust.

After marching out of Atlanta in mid-November, General William Tecumseh Sherman's stretching army arrived in Savannah in December of 1864. His annihilating 300-mile "March to the Sea" had resulted in the burnings of both government and private property. Sherman's immense army of approximately 60,000 men began flowing into South Carolina in January. As these hardened forces crossed the Savannah River, certain district governments in South Carolina prudently decided to relocate their records for safe keeping. Gillisonville, located 36 miles north of Bluffton by stagecoach route, had been the seat of Beaufort District since 1840, housing all vital records. While en route to Columbia, these local government documents were consequently intercepted by Sherman's troops. As a result, many of the district's official papers were burned.

As Sherman's battle-tested army trekked north towards Columbia, they encountered moderate Confederate resistance at Rivers Bridge on the Salkehatchie River. On February 3, two Union brigades flanked the river's primary crossing and waded through the murky swamp, where a battle thus ensued. The Rebels, commanded by Major-General Lafayette McLaws, were forced to withdraw from their earthworks after a tough contest. The Confederates ultimately suffered 170 casualties compared to the North's estimated 92 killed, wounded, or missing.[28]

The opposition only delayed Sherman's powerful right wing momentarily. The Federal brigades continued marching north, reaching Columbia on February 17 as Southern forces hastily retreated from the city. A considerable sector of the capitol was subsequently destroyed by fire; although Sherman denied accusations that his soldiers kindled the initial spark. As the searing firestorm was rapidly spreading throughout downtown Columbia, the Confederates were simultaneously evacuating Charleston. The state of South Carolina was in turmoil and defeat loomed over the South.

Chapter VII Source Notes

1. *Charleston Mercury*, June 6, 1863.

2. Official Records of the Union and Confederate Armies, Series 1, Volume 14 (Washington, D.C.: Government Printing Office, 1894–1922), 309.

3. *Richmond Dispatch*, June 6, 1863.

4. *Official Records of the Union and Confederate Armies, Series 1, Volume 14* (Washington, D.C.: Government Printing Office, 1894–1922), 314.

5. Abraham J. Palmer, D.D., *The History of the Forty-Eighth Regiment, New York State Volunteers in the War of the Union 1861–1865* (Brooklyn, N.Y.: Veterans Association of the Regiment. 1885), 46.

6. "Intelligence in the Civil War," "Black Dispatches" Central Intelligence Agency. https://www.cia.gov/library/publications/additional-publications/civil-war/p20.htm

7. Francis H. Casstevens, *Edward A. Wild and the African Brigade in the Civil War* (Jefferson, N.C.: McFarland & Company, Inc. Publishers, 2003), 62.

8. *Official Records of the Union and Confederate Armies, Series 1, Volume 14, Part I* (Washington, D.C.: Government Printing Office, 1894–1922), 463.

9. Louis P. Masur, *The Civil War: A Concise History* (New York, N.Y.: Oxford University Press, 2011), 40.

10. Abraham J. Palmer, D.D., *The History of the Forty-Eighth Regiment, New York State Volunteers in the War of the Union 1861–1865* (Brooklyn, N.Y.: Veterans Association of the Regiment. 1885), 72.

11. *Official Records of the Union and Confederate Armies, Series 1, Volume 14* (Washington, D.C.: Government Printing Office, 1894–1922), 469.

12. *Official Records of the Union and Confederate Navies, Series 1, Volume 14* (Washington, D.C.: Government Printing Office, 1894–1922), 237.

13. *Official Records of the Union and Confederate Navies, Series 1, Volume 14* Washington, D.C.: Government Printing Office, 1894–1922), 237.

14. Message of the President of the United States including the Report of the Secretary of the Navy, December 7, 1863, "Expedition against Bluffton, South Carolina" (Washington, D.C.: Government Printing Office, 1863), 219.

15. H.G. Wells, *A Short History of the World* (New York, N.Y.: Cosimo, Inc., 2005, and The Review Corporation Publishers & The Macmillan Company, 1922), 388.

16. *"The Civil War" Part 2*, in collaboration with Henry Steele Commager, Ph.D. Encyclopedia Britannica Films, Inc.

17. *Official Records of the Union and Confederate Armies, Series 1, Volume 28* (Washington, D.C.: Government Printing Office, 1894–1922), 11.

18. *Official Records of the Union and Confederate Armies, Series 1, Volume 28* (Washington, D.C.: Government Printing Office, 1894–1922), 11.

19. *Official Records of the Union and Confederate Armies, Series 1, Volume 28* (Washington, D.C.: Government Printing Office, 1894–1922), 21.

20. Luis F. Emilio, *The Assault on Fort Wagner, July 18, 1863* (Boston, MA: Rand Avery Company, The Franklin Press, 1887), 12.

21. Abraham J. Palmer, D.D., *The History of the Forty-Eighth Regiment, New York State Volunteers in the War of the Union 1861–1865* (Brooklyn, N.Y.: Veterans Association of the Regiment. 1885), 107.

22. *Official Records of the Union and Confederate Armies, Series 1, Volume 28, Part 1* (Washington, D.C.: Government Printing Office, 1894–1922), 210.

23. John G. Abbott's Diary, August 7, 1863.

24. Luis M. Evans, *So Rudely Sepulchered: The 48th New York Volunteer Infantry Regiment During the Campaign for Charleston, July 1863* (Fort Leavenworth, KS: U.S. Army Command and General Staff College, 2000), 89.

25. Luis M. Evans, *So Rudely Sepulchered: The 48th New York Volunteer Infantry Regiment During the Campaign for Charleston, July 1863* (Fort Leavenworth, KS: U.S. Army Command and General Staff College, 2000), 89.

26. Gettysburg Address, November 19, 1863.

27. H. David Stone, *Vital Rails: The Charleston & Savannah Railroad and the Civil War in Coastal South Carolina* (Columbia S.C.: University of South Carolina Press, 2008), 224.

28. Rivers Bridge Battle Summary, National Park Service, www.cr.nps.gov/hps/abpp/battles/sc011.htm.

VIII

Conclusion

After abandoning Richmond in the spring, "General Robert E. Lee was determined to make one last attempt to escape the closing Union pincers and reach his supplies at Lynchburg."[1] His retreat, however, was thwarted by Northern forces. On April 9, 1865, Lee reluctantly surrendered to General Ulysses S. Grant at Appomattox Court House. The Army of Northern Virginia was thus officially disbanded on April 12, ending all hopes for a Confederate victory and independence. The surrender of Lee's army heralded the conclusion of the war.

Together, the Union's army and navy had split the South in two halves along the Mississippi River. Sherman's forces had carved a fiery swath from Atlanta to Savannah before turning north and tramping through the Carolinas. The Confederate army was overcome and the Southern coastline was under a strangulating blockade. Southern cotton exports had plunged from nearly three million bales in 1861 to only a trickle by 1865. Critical imports needed to sustain the Rebels were almost non-existent. Crops throughout the South were severely depleted. With the Confederacy in economic ruin and its military routed, victory belonged to the North.

Most estimates place the aggregate sum of men who died in the war at roughly 620,000. This inconceivable figure includes deaths from battle, disease, and illness. Of the troops who perished, 360,000 men in blue paid the ultimate sacrifice, while 260,000 gray-clad soldiers never returned home.[2] Of the survivors, several hundred thousand staggered home wounded to either side of the Mason-Dixon Line.

The War Between the States was a tragedy unequalled in American history. Perhaps H.G. Wells best placed this immense saga into perspective when he spoke of the unprecedented growth of the United States. He concluded that America had grown at an unparalleled rate until it finally became one of the greatest empires to ever exist. "But on the way to this present greatness and security the American people passed through one phase of dire conflict."[3] According to Wells, the epic story of the American Civil War was a tragedy that America has never experienced before or after, resulting in "...a terrible waste and killing of men."[4]

Upon the Confederacy's demise, antebellum Bluffton vanished forever, and with it the social order of the planter class and the institution of slavery. "After the war, with their homes burned, their Hilton Head plantations confiscated by the Federal government, and their rice plantations along the New and Savannah Rivers in ruin, many were bankrupt by the war and their Bluffton properties were sold for taxes."[5]

Lee surrenders to Grant at Appomattox Court House. Courtesy of the Appomattox Court House National Historic Park.

Fortunately for the efforts of historic preservation and the intrinsic value of Bluffton's National Register Historic District, ten antebellum buildings of splendid architectural design continue to grace Old Town with their charming presence. Perhaps of even greater historical consequence is the natural existence of the sprawling and magnificent Secession Oak, which unfailingly weathered those tempestuous times of war, and still stands resolute today.

From the period when the community's first dwellings were constructed in the early 1800s, through its incorporation in 1852, to the contemporary era, the burning of Bluffton in 1863 may be the most salient and influential episode in the annals of town history. On a far grander scale, *The Bluffton Expedition* recounts merely a brief, yet significant chapter, bound deep within the numerous and lengthy volumes of the American Civil War.

Chapter VIII Source Notes

1. Appomattox Court House Battle Summary, National Park Service, www.nps.gov/hps/abpp/battles/va097.htm

2. Steven E. Woodworth, *This Great Struggle: America's Civil War* (Lanham, MD: Rowman and Littlefield Publishers, Inc., 2011), 377.

3. H.G. Wells, *A Short History of the World* (New York, N.Y.: Cosimo, Inc., 2005; The Review Corporation Publishers & The Macmillan Company, 1922), 384.

4. H.G. Wells, *A Short History of the World* (New York, N.Y.: Cosimo, Inc., 2005; The Review Corporation Publishers & The Macmillan Company, 1922), 265.

5. *A Longer Short History of Bluffton, South Carolina* (Bluffton, S.C.: Bluffton Historical Preservation Society, Inc., 1988), 9.

Bibliography

Abbott, John G. Diary from the 48th New York Regiment.

americancivilwar.com/statepic/south_carolina.html

Ballard, Ted. *Battle of First Bull Run*. Washington: Center of Military History, United States Army, 2004.

Baxley, Neil. Letter to Jeff Fulgham, August 9, 2011.

Baxley, Neil. *No Prouder Fate: The Story of the 11th South Carolina Volunteer Infantry*. Bloomington, IN: AuthorHouse, 2005.

Behan, William A. *A Short History of Callawassie Island, South Carolina: The Lives and Times of Its Owners and Residents, 1711–1985*. Lincoln, NE: iUniverse, 2004.

Bradford, Sarah. *Harriet Tubman: The Moses of Her People*. Bedford, MA: Applewood Books, 1886.

Burn, Billie. *An Island Named Daufuskie*. Spartanburg, S.C.: The Reprint Company, Publishers, 1991.

Casstevens, Francis H. Edward A. *Wild and the African Brigade in the Civil War.* Jefferson, N.C.: McFarland & Company, Inc. Publishers, 2003.

Charleston Mercury, June 6, 1863.

Cisco, Walter Bryan. *Henry Timrod: a Biography.* Cranbury: Rosemont Publishing and Printing Corp. Associated University Presses, 2004.

"The Civil War." Encyclopedia Britannica Films, Inc., in collaboration with Henry Steele Commager, Ph.D.

Coffman, Richard M., and Kurt D. Graham. *To Honor These Men: A History of the Phillips Georgia Legion Infantry Battalion.* Macon, GA: Mercer University Press, 2007.

Confederate War Journal, Volume 2. New York and Lexington, KY: April, 1894.

Congressional Report No. 2584. House of Representatives, 51st Congress, 1st Session. Washington, D.C.: June 27, 1890.

Davis, William C. *Rhett: The Turbulent Life and Times of a Fire Eater.* Columbia: University of South Carolina Press, 2001.

"The Day the Big Gun Shoot." *The State.* Columbia, S.C. September 24, 2011.

Dictionary of American Naval Fighting Ships (DANFS)
http://www.history.navy.mil/danfs/c12/commod ore_mcdonough.htm

Emancipation Proclamation of January 1, 1863.

Emilio, Luis F. *The Assault on Fort Wagner*, July 18, 1863. Boston, MA: Rand Avery Company, The Franklin Press, 1887.

Evans, Luis M. *So Rudely Sepulchered: The 48th New York Volunteer Infantry Regiment During the Campaign for Charleston, July 1863.* Fort Leavenworth, KS: U.S. Army Command and General Staff College, 2000.

Fort Sumter National Monument, Exhibit Text, February 2002. National Park Service. Visitor Education Center, Liberty Square, Charleston, S.C.

Gettysburg Address, November 19, 1863.

Greer, Margaret. *The Sands of Time: A History of Hilton Head Island.* Hilton Head, S.C.: SouthArt, Inc., 1989.

A Guide to Historic Bluffton. Bluffton, S.C.: The Bluffton Historical Preservation Society, Inc., 2007.

Halliburton, Lloyd. *Saddle Soldiers: The Civil War Correspondence of General William Stokes of the 4th South Carolina Cavalry.* Orangeburg, S.C.: Sandlapper Publishing Company, Inc., 1993.

"Intelligence in the Civil War," "Black Dispatches." Central Intelligence Agency. https://www.cia.gov/library/publications/additional-publications/civil-war/p20.htm

Jones, Robert S. Jr. "Going to the Salt," *Coastal Angler Magazine*, January 2011.

Jones, Robert S. Jr. "Saltworks in the Lowcountry," *Coastal Angler Magazine*, December 2010.

Kennedy, David M., Elizabeth Cohen and Thomas A. Bailey. *The American Pageant, Volume 1, To 1877*. Boston, MA: Houghton Mifflin Company, 2006.

Lattimore, Ralston B. National Park Service,

Historical Handbook, Series No. 18. Washington, D.C., 1954.

A Longer Short History of Bluffton, South Carolina. Bluffton, S.C.: Bluffton Historical Preservation Society, Inc., 1988.

Masur, Louis P. *The Civil War: A Concise History*. New York, N.Y.: Oxford University Press, 2011.

McNeese, Tim. *America's Civil War*. Dayton, OH: Milliken Publishing Company, 2003.

Message of the President of the United States including the Report of the Secretary of the Navy, December 7, 1863. "Expedition against Bluffton, South Carolina," Washington, D.C.: Government Printing Office, 1863.

Miller, Edward A. *Lincoln's Abolitionist General: The Biography of David Hunter*. Columbia, S.C.: University of South Carolina Press, 1997.

Moore, Frank, Ed. *The Rebellion Record: A Diary of American Events, Volume 4.* New York, N.Y.: G.P Putnam. 1862.

Nichols, James M. *Perry's Saints: or The Fighting Parsons Regiment in the War of the Rebellion.* Boston, MA: D. Lothrop and Company, 1886.

Oates, Stephen B. *With Malice Toward None: A Life of Abraham Lincoln.* New York, N.Y.: HarperCollins, 1977.

Official Records of the Union and Confederate Armies, Series 1, Volume 6. Washington, D.C.: Government Printing Office, 1894–1922.

Official Records of the Union and Confederate Armies, Series 1, Volume 14. Washington, D.C. Government Printing Office, 1894–1922.

Official Records of the Union and Confederate Armies, Series 1, Volume 28. Washington, D.C.: Government Printing Office, 1894–1922.

Official Records of the Union and Confederate Navies, Series 1, Volume 12. Washington, D.C.: Government Printing Office, 1894–1922.

Official Records of the Union and Confederate Navies, Series 1, Volume 14. Washington, D.C.: Government Printing Office, 1894–1922.

Palmer, Abraham J., D.D. *The History of the Forty-Eighth Regiment, New York State Volunteers in the War of the Union 1861–1865.* Brooklyn, N.Y.: Veterans Association of the Regiment, 1885.

Richmond Dispatch, June 6, 1863.

Rivers Bridge Battle Summary, National Park Service.   www.cr.nps.gov/hps/abpp/battles/sc011.htm

Rowland, Lawrence S., Alexander Moore and George C. Rogers Jr. *The History of Beaufort County, South Carolina: Volume 1, 1514–1861.* Columbia, S.C.: University of South Carolina Press, 1996.

Second Inaugural Address. March 4, 1865.

A Short History of the Early Days of Bluffton, South Carolina. Bluffton, S.C.: Bluffton Historical Preservation Society, Inc., 1983.

Sinha, Manisha. *Slavery in the United States: A Social, Political, and Historical Encyclopedia, Volume One.* Edited by Junius P. Rodriguez. Santa Barbara: ABC CLIO, Inc., 2007.

Smith, Henry. "The Baronies of South Carolina,"

The South Carolina Historical and Genealogical Magazine. Volume 13, July, 1912, Number 3.

Snowden, Yates, and H.G. Cutler. *History of South Carolina, Volume 2.* Chicago and New York: The Lewis Publishing Company, 1930.

Southern Ports Blockade Proclamations, April 19, 27, 1861.

Stone, H. David. *Vital Rails: The Charleston & Savannah Railroad and the Civil War in Coastal South Carolina.* Columbia, S.C.: University of South Carolina Press, 2008.

Sweetman, Jack. *American Naval History: An Illustrated Chronology of the U.S. Navy and Marine Corps, 1775–Present.* Annapolis, MD: Naval Institute Press, 2002.

Tomblin, Barbara. *Bluejackets and Contrabands: African Americans and the Union Navy.* Lexington, KY: The University Press of Kentucky, 2009.

Wells, H.G. *A Short History of the World.* New York, N.Y.: Cosimo, Inc., 2005. Originally published by The Review Corporation Publishers & The Macmillan Company, 1922.

Woodward, C. Vann. *Mary Chesnut's Civil War.* New Haven, CT: Yale, 1981.

Woodworth, Steven E. *This Great Struggle: America's Civil War.* Lanham MD: Rowman and Littlefield Publishers, Inc., 2011.